BASS

5-STRING
ETUDES, RIFFS, SONGS & EXERCISES
NATE NAVARRO

Message from the Author

Hey, Nate here. I'm so excited to help you in your pursuit to become a better 5-string bass player! Whether you're brand new to playing the bass, or you're a seasoned professional, this book is for YOU. I've included a ton of playing styles and a wide variety of musical and technical exercises which will help prepare you for any musical situation you find yourself in, and for whatever musical path you choose to follow.

Peace,

Nate Navarro

About the Author

Nate Navarro is a bassist, educator, and content creator living in Nashville, Tennessee. A Berklee College of Music graduate and in-demand professional bassist, he has recorded with multi-platinum producers, toured over 30 countries, and played on recordings with incredible musicians including Devin Townsend, Steven Wilson, Steve Vai, Gavin Harrison, Marko Minnemann, Mike Keneally, Morgan Ågren, Chad Kroeger, and many others.

He is endorsed by dozens of the music industry's top companies including Fender, Kiesel, Spector, Genzler Amplification, PRS, ESP, Mayones, Dingwall, NS Design, D'Addarío, Darkglass, Electro-Harmonix and others. He has had over 100 in-person music students, and has performed as a music-product demonstrator across the globe. You can find him on YouTube, where he has over 280k subscribers and 70 million views.

Table of Contents

Navarro Music LLC
All rights reserved - International Copyright Secured

MODERATE to ADVANCED

Lessons *continued...*

Advanced Picking Techniques

Riffs & Etudes

MODERATE to ADVANCED
Riffs & Etudes *continued...*

Table of Contents

MODERATE to ADVANCED
Songs
Additional Online Learning Materials

How to Use This Book

Video

As you read through this book, follow along with the Official *Bass 5-String Etudes, Riffs, Songs & Exercises* **VIDEO**. It contains close-up demonstrations, listening examples, play-alongs, and additional exercises for all of the material in this book. The video content is extremely helpful in learning the material thoroughly, and without forming bad technical habits. I will be active in the comments section, answering questions you might have. Watch here:

URL: https://youtu.be/_CR8I6CiOOQ

QR Code:

Get Your Files

Supplemental *Audio Examples*, *Bassless Backing Tracks*, and *Guitar Pro* files are included with the purchase of this book. Download them here:

URL: https://bit.ly/5-String_Downloads

QR Code:

Hashtag

Share your progress! Use #natenavarrobassbook on social media.
I'll drop a comment if I see you. :)

Beginner Lessons

Introduction

Welcome! Learning to play the bass guitar, or any musical instrument, can be an incredibly rewarding pursuit. Studies show profound physical, emotional, and cognitive benefits in people who practice or perform regularly, and I'm grateful to have witnessed many times the power that music holds in creating adventurous opportunities and fruitful relationships.

The bass was my instrument of choice initially because I loved its sound and the visceral feeling of hitting the strings and getting a thunderous sound from the amplifier. Playing the instrument that inspires people to move on the dance floor or in the mosh pit is exhilarating.

But before we head out on tour, there's some ground work we need to cover. The Beginner section of this book will lay a firm foundation for the fun ahead.

Be sure to watch the Official *Bass 5-String Etudes, Riffs, Songs & Exercises* **VIDEO** as you read through this book. I'm a proponent of having video lessons for guidance, especially in the early stages, because students often develop bad habits in their form when relying on books alone. They say *a picture is worth a thousand words...* I feel better as a teacher providing you with multiple angles at 24 frames per second. Watch here:

URL: https://youtu.be/_CR8I6CiOOQ?t=27

QR Code:

The Parts of the Bass

Video
https://youtu.be/_CR8I6CiOOQ?t=70

Knowing the parts of the bass will enable us to more effectively communicate basic concepts, such as holding the bass, different techniques, tuning, dialing in tone, and more.

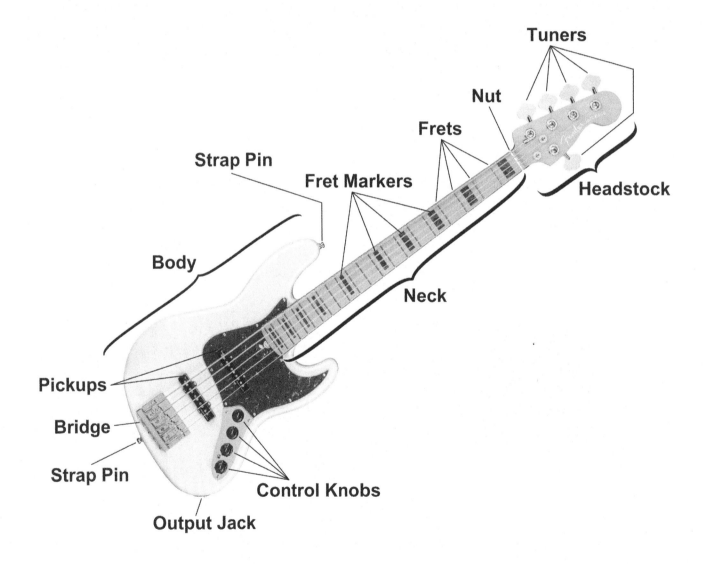

How to Hold the Bass

Video 🎥

https://youtu.be/_CR8I6CiOOQ?t=115

Holding the bass properly will allow you to play longer and prevent strain.
Let's cover two ways to hold the bass when sitting, and then we'll go over proper strap height for standing.

The Casual Posture
Rest the curve of the lower body on your right leg.
Have the back of the bass snug against your torso.
Rest your right forearm lightly on the body, with your fingers just over the strings.
Press your left thumb against the back of the neck, and rest your fingers on the strings.
The headstock should be elevated, and both of your wrists should be straight and relaxed.

The Classical Posture
Rest the curve of the lower body on your left leg.
Elevate the headstock slightly higher.
Your left and right arm positions will be similar to the Casual Posture.
The Classical Posture gives you easier access to the upper neck region.

Standing

Put your head and right arm through the strap so that it rests on your left shoulder.
I suggest using a strap with a minimum width of 2.5" (6.35 cm) for better support.
The bass should hang in a position that keeps your wrists straight and relaxed.

If your left wrist is flexing upward uncomfortably, the bass might be too low. If your right wrist is flexing downward uncomfortably, the bass is either too high, or you need to lift your forearm.

Take some time to find the perfect strap length because it makes a big difference in preventing strain.

Navarro Music LLC

Tuning

Video 📹

https://youtu.be/_CR8I6CiOOQ?t=202

If your bass is out of tune it won't sound right, and there are many factors that can affect your tuning, such as temperature, humidity, the strings settling in, taking your bass in and out of its case; so be sure to tune often.

The 5-string bass is tuned **B E A D G**. Watch the video, linked above, to tune with me and learn a few tips.

Intro to Fingerstyle

Video

https://youtu.be/_CR8I6CiOOQ?t=312

Fingerstyle is the most common way of playing the bass, and the technique itself has been used on other instruments for millennia. Proper form can get a little deep, because at many times, in addition to plucking a string, you will simultaneously mute other strings with a combination of both hands. Watch the video linked above for an in depth walkthrough of the following exercises.

Intro to Fingerstyle
Exercises 1 through 5
Nate Navarro

Intro to Fingerstyle
Exercise 6
Nate Navarro

Standard tuning

♩ = 84

Exercise 6

Intro to Fingerstyle

Exercises 7 through 8
Nate Navarro

Standard tuning

♩ = 84

Exercise 7

Exercise 8

Intro to Fingerstyle

Exercise 9
Nate Navarro

Navarro Music LLC

How to Read Tabs

Video

https://youtu.be/_CR8I6CiOOQ?t=953

Tabs, or tablature, is a form of music notation that enables you to start practicing songs and exercises very quickly. Its simplicity can leave a bit to be desired in terms of musicality, but we're not going to worry about that for now. We just want to hit the ground running with some riffs and practice the mechanics of our instrument.

When your bass is laid flat, it looks like this...
The B string is at the bottom, followed by the E, A, D, and G strings. Tablature is laid out the same way. We have five lines, and each of them represent one string of the bass. B, E, A, D, and G. If we assign a number to each fret, we can then point out any note in any position of the bass guitar. For example, the open string is zero, the first fret is one, the second fret is two, and so on... all the way up the neck.

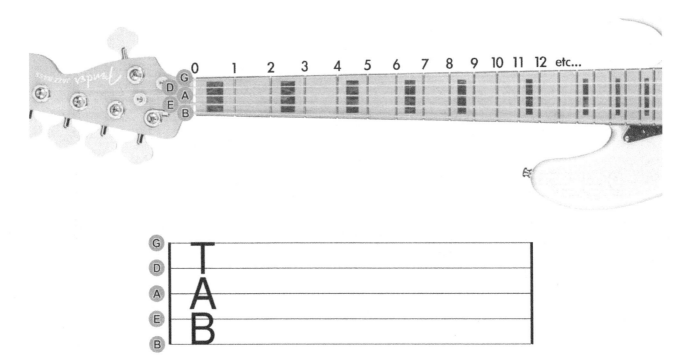

18

If we see a five on the second line, we know to play the fifth fret on the E string.

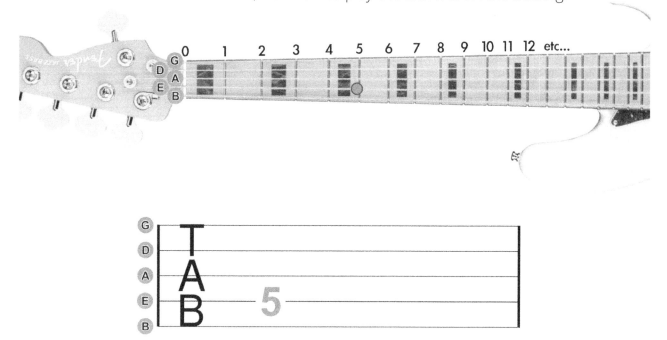

If we see a 12 on the third line, we know to play the 12th fret on the A string.

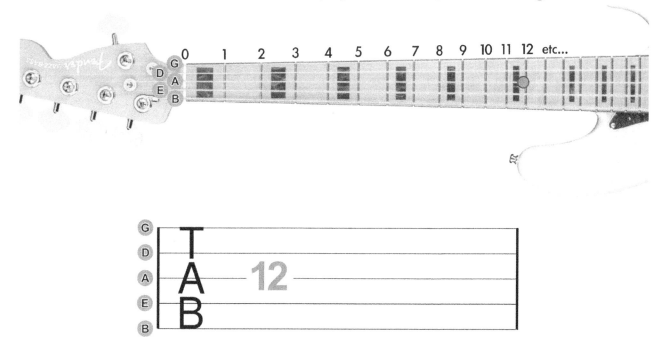

Navarro Music LLC

Now here's where the fun comes in... If we string a few of these numbers together, and read them left to right, we can start making music.

Take a look at this bass line. Can we make sense of it?

Watch the video linked at the beginning of this section for further guidance on playing this bass line, and to jam along with the band!

Navarro Music LLC

Intro to Slap

Video
https://youtu.be/_CR8I6CiOOQ?t=1126

The motion used for slapping is similar to the dance move that we all know and love, "Jazz Hands." The motion begins at the elbow, while the shoulder remains still. The hand pivots around its centerpoint and the wrist and thumb remain straight and relaxed. As you perform your Jazz Hand, bring it down to the bass and allow your thumb to slap against the B string.

Follow the link above for a close, multi-angle look at the slap technique. We will also go through the exercises on the following pages. Don't forget to bring your bass face.

Intro to Slap
Exercises 1 through 4
Nate Navarro

Navarro Music LLC

Beginner Riffs & Etudes

Video

https://youtu.be/_CR8I6CiOOQ?t=1732

Latin Blues
Beginner Example 1
Nate Navarro

Gojishuggah
Beginner Example 2
Nate Navarro

Navarro Music LLC

Fretting-Hand Shifting

Beginner Example 3
Nate Navarro

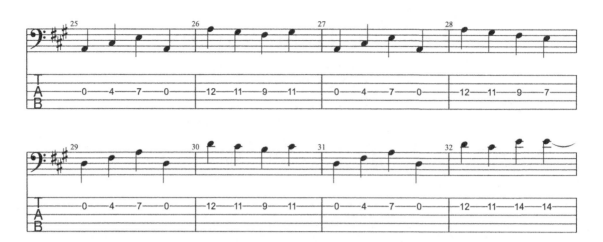

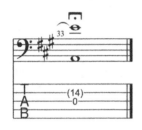

Navarro Music LLC

Scalar Etude
Beginner Example 4
Nate Navarro

Navarro Music LLC

Just Wanna Know

Beginner Example 5
Nate Navarro

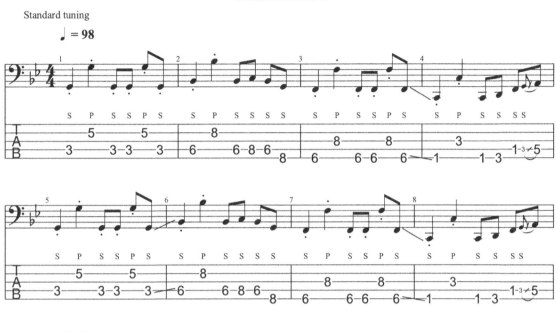

Navarro Music LLC

Low Drone
Beginner Example 6
Nate Navarro

Fiesta
Beginner Example 7
Nate Navarro

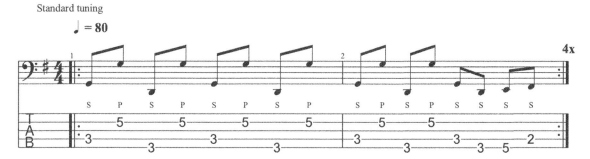

Navarro Music LLC

Arpeggiation
Beginner Example 8
Nate Navarro

Navarro Music LLC

Finger Independence

Video

https://youtu.be/_CR8I6CiOOQ?t=2152

The following exercise breaks down all of the chromatic combinations you'll find in a one-finger-per-fret, four-notes-per-string system. It will help limber up your fretting hand and get those neurons firing. Practice along with the linked video, and set the video's speed to faster or slower, to match your current pace.

15. Ring, Middle, Index, Pinky

Finger Independence
Exercise 1
Nate Navarro

Finger Independence Exercise 2

Exercise 2
Nate Navarro

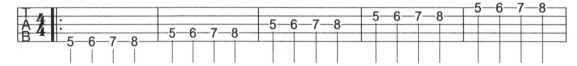

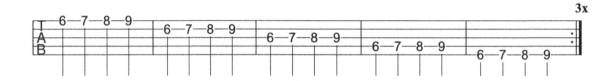

Finger Independence Exercise 3

Exercise 3
Nate Navarro

Standard tuning

♩ = 89

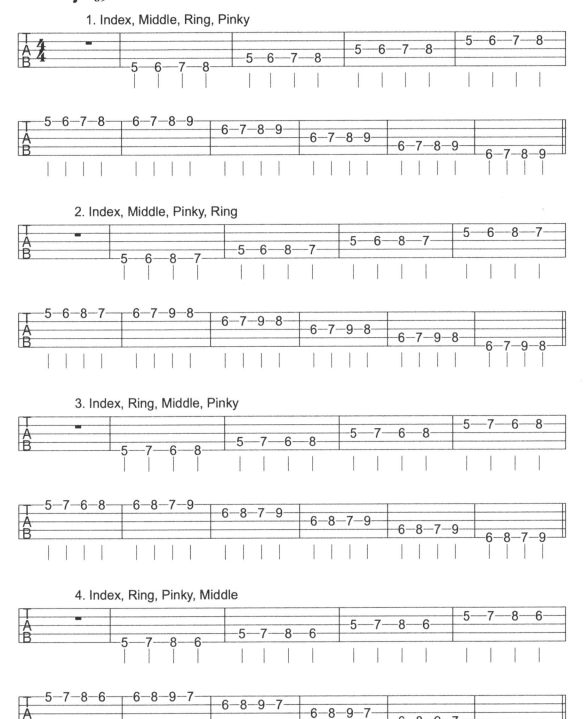

1. Index, Middle, Ring, Pinky

2. Index, Middle, Pinky, Ring

3. Index, Ring, Middle, Pinky

4. Index, Ring, Pinky, Middle

Navarro Music LLC

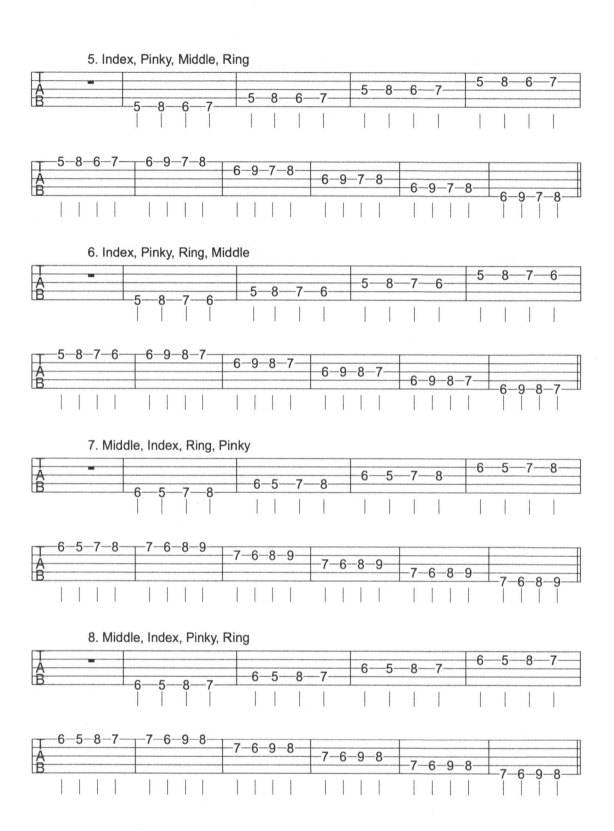

5. Index, Pinky, Middle, Ring

6. Index, Pinky, Ring, Middle

7. Middle, Index, Ring, Pinky

8. Middle, Index, Pinky, Ring

Exercises - Beginner

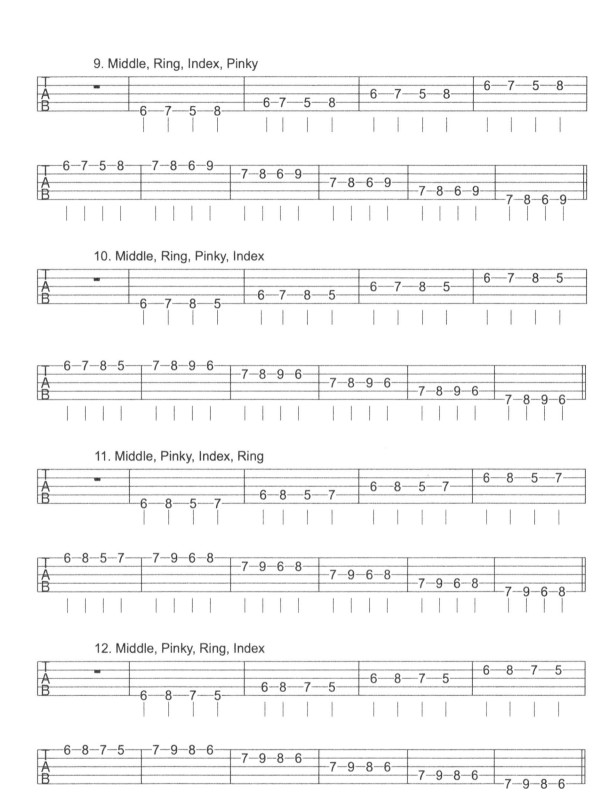

9. Middle, Ring, Index, Pinky

10. Middle, Ring, Pinky, Index

11. Middle, Pinky, Index, Ring

12. Middle, Pinky, Ring, Index

Exercises - Beginner

Navarro Music LLC

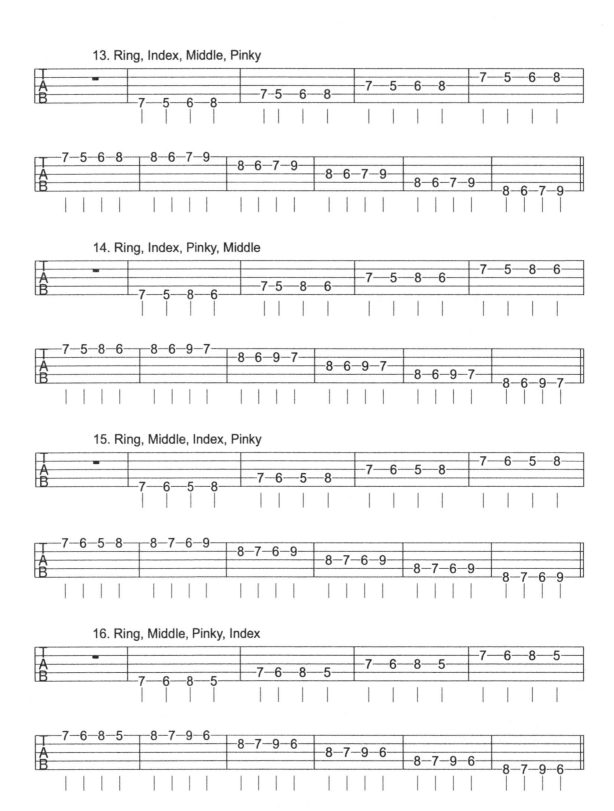

17. Ring, Pinky, Index, Middle

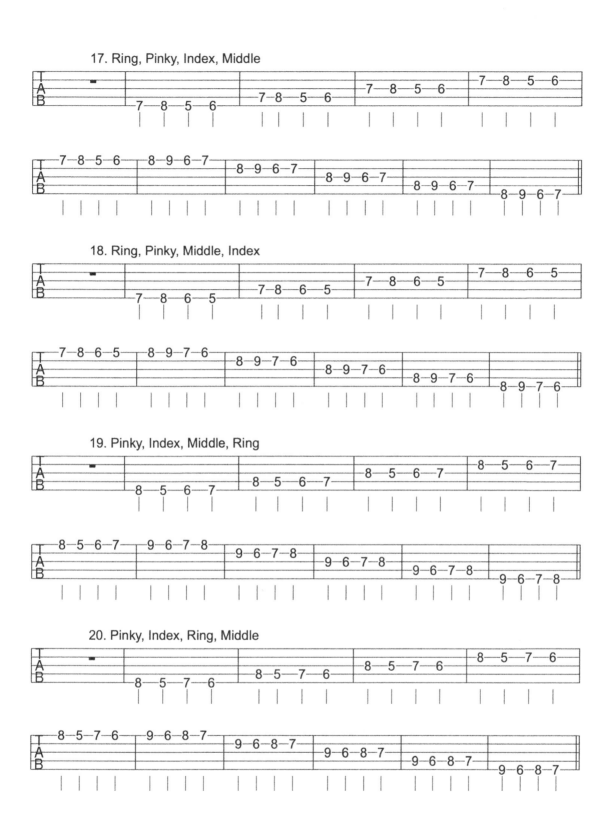

18. Ring, Pinky, Middle, Index

19. Pinky, Index, Middle, Ring

20. Pinky, Index, Ring, Middle

Exercises - Beginner

Navarro Music LLC

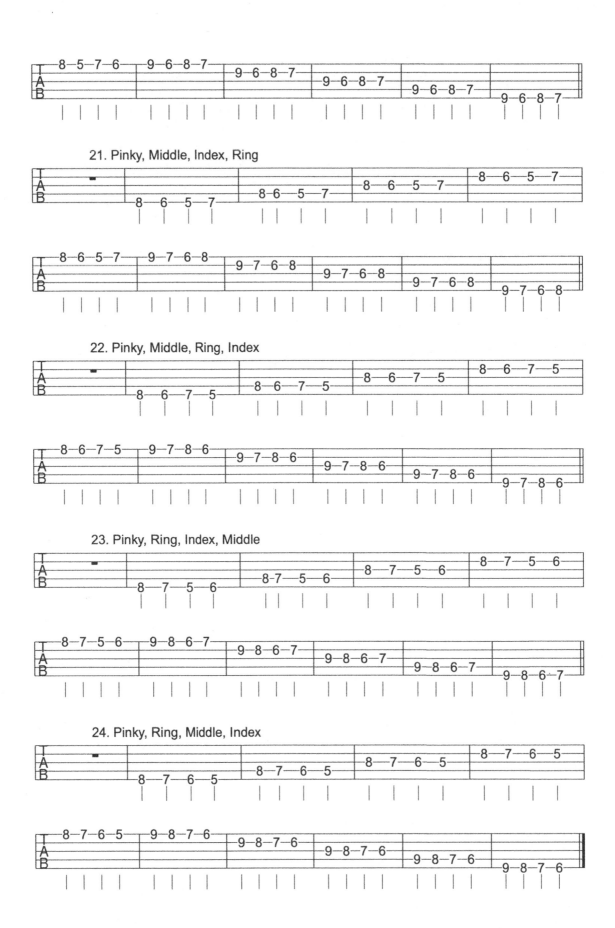

21. Pinky, Middle, Index, Ring

22. Pinky, Middle, Ring, Index

23. Pinky, Ring, Index, Middle

24. Pinky, Ring, Middle, Index

How to Write a Bass Line

Video 🎥
https://youtu.be/_CR8I6CiOOQ?t=4231

Imagine this.... you're in a band, and your guitarist comes up with a sick riff. It's now your job to come up with a bass line that compliments his ideas while holding down the low end and locking in with the drummer.

There is not one "right" way to do this - You have creative decisions to make tonally, harmonically, rhythmically, and in embellishment. Let's explore the latter three in this exercise. Be sure to watch the associated video to hear guitarist, Kris Barocsi's riff, and check out his channel for more sick riffs and great guitar content: https://www.youtube.com/user/falden82

Lessons -
Moderate to Advanced

Navarro Music LLC

Terms to know for Example 1...

Root Note - The first note in a chord.
> *Example:* G is the root note of a G Major chord. A is the root note of an A minor chord.

Example 1: Root Notes

In popular music, simplicity is often king, especially when it comes to bass lines. Example 1 takes a familiar *root-note-pulse* approach, following the chord changes exactly, while playing steady 16th notes.

Remember, our goal in this context is to compliment Kris' riff, hold down the low end, and lock in with the drummer. While simple, this bass line accomplishes all three goals, and it definitely won't get you fired from the gig. ;)

How To Write A Bass Line

Example 1: Root Notes
Nate Navarro ft Kris Barocsi

Standard tuning

♩ = 98

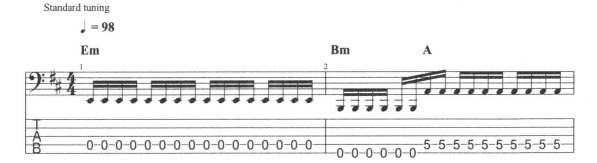

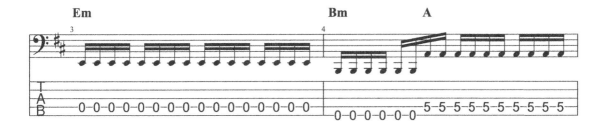

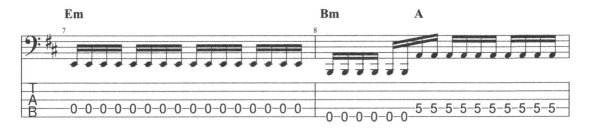

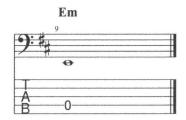

Navarro Music LLC

Lessons -
Moderate to Advanced

Terms to know for Example 2...

Space - Also referred to as "rest," the absence of sound for a defined period of time.
Example: The sections between bass notes in the intro of "Crazy Train" by Ozzy Osbourne.

Syncopation - Diverging from regular metrical accents, usually emphasizing weak beats.
Example: The intro hits of "Come On Come Over" by Jaco Pastorius.

Example 2: Space & Syncopation

Space & Syncopation can add excitement and energy to a song, and help provide contrast to other sections. For the best effect, multiple musicians should play these parts together - Notice how the kick drum follows the bass part of Example 2 more closely than it follows the bass part of Example 1. If the kick were playing the original pattern, it would be much less impactful. Locking in with your bandmates and nailing those hits is a rewarding feeling, and it's an effective way to get the crowd moving.

How To Write A Bass Line

Example 2: Space & Syncopation

Nate Navarro ft Kris Barocsi

Navarro Music LLC
All rights reserved - International Copyright Secured

Terms to know for Example 3...

Diatonic - In melody and harmony, the exclusive use of notes within a given key.
Example: Using any note of the C Major scale while playing in the key of C Major.

Non-Diatonic - In melody and harmony, incorporating notes outside of the key.
Example: Using the notes C#, D#, F#, G#, or A# while playing in the key of C Major.

Parallel Keys - Keys beginning with the same note, but having different key signatures.
Example: C Major, C Dorian, C Phrygian, C Lydian, C Mixolydian, C Aeolian, C Locrian.

Chord Tones - Notes that exist within a certain chord.
Example: In an A minor chord, the chord tones are A, C and E.

Scale Tones - Notes that exist within a certain scale.
Example: In an A minor scale, the scale tones are A, B, C, D, E, F, and G.

Lessons -
Moderate to Advanced

Navarro Music LLC
All rights reserved - International Copyright Secured

Example 3: Harmonic Inversion & Modal Interchange

Harmonic Inversion uses non-root chord tones to change the quality of a chord. For example, the second chord in Kris' riff is B minor (B, D, F#). Most often a B note will be played by the bass to support this chord. Alternatively, we can play chord tones D or F# to invert the harmony.

If a D note is played by the bass during a B minor chord, that chord is called "B minor over D," written Bmin/D. The D note is the second note of the chord (B, **D**, F#), making it the first option, sequentially, for inversion. Because of this, the chord is considered to be in *first inversion*, and may be referred to as B minor in first inversion. In Example 3, B minor in first inversion occurs in measures 4 and 8.

If an F# note is played by the bass during a B minor chord, that chord is called "B minor over F#," written Bmin/F#. Given that the F# note is the third note in the chord (B, D, **F#**), and the second option sequentially for inversion, the chord is also called B minor in second inversion. In Example 3, B minor in second inversion occurs at measure 6.

In the second half of measures 4 and 8 we see written A/C#, spoken A over C#; *A* is short for *A Major*. The chord tones are A, C# and E, and we are playing a C# in the bass, giving us, "A over C#," or, A Major in first inversion. Notice how changing the inversion of a chord affects its tonal character.

Harmonic inversion is an excellent way to add variation to an arrangement, or lead into new sections of a song. In some progressions, inverting chords allows the bass line to ascend or descend in a stepwise fashion, which can sound very pleasing. Study the E dorian *Harmonic Inversion Guide* on the following page, then experiment with a few inversions of your own using the bassless backing track. Write down a few of your ideas on the page following the Harmonic Inversion Guide.

Navarro Music LLC

Harmonic Inversion Guide
Inversions in the key of E dorian
Nate Navarro

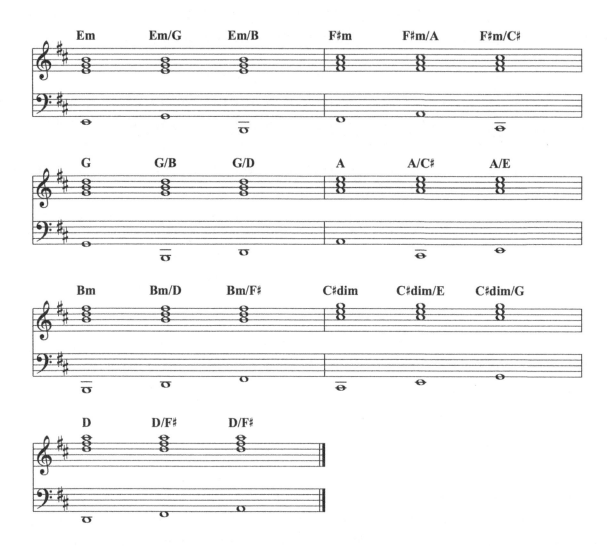

Harmonic Inversion Practice

We have established that Kris' riff is in the key of E Dorian, which includes the notes E, F#, G, A, B, C#, and D. When stacking these scale tones in thirds, we get the following diatonic chords:

E minor (E, G, B)
F# minor (F#, A, C#)
G Major (G, B, D)
A Major (A, C#, E)
B minor (B, D, F#)
C# diminished (C#, E, G)
D Major (D, F#, A)

Modal Interchange allows us to use non-diatonic chords from parallel keys. For example, the first chord of Kris' riff is E minor (E, G, B). Most commonly, the bass will play an E note to support this chord. Alternatively, through modal interchange, a C note can be played to change the chord to a C Major 7 (C, E, G, B). The result is a more complex and beautiful sound. The complexity comes from the non-diatonic C note, and beauty comes from the character of the Major 7 chord.

While C Major 7 is not naturally found in E Dorian, it *is* found in the parallel key of E Aeolian (also known as, E minor). In this instance of Modal Interchange, we are *borrowing* non-diatonic harmony, *the C Major 7*, from the key of E Aeolian, and applying to the key of E Dorian. In Example 3, this occurs in measures 1, 3, and 7.

Try finding a few modal interchange textures of your own, using the *Modal Interchange Guide* on the following page, and the bassless backing track. The *Modal Interchange Guide* lists all harmonies that may be borrowed from parallel modes. If this music theory is a bit beyond your experience, no worries at all. Instead, try finding a few non-diatonic notes that work well at some point in the riff. In E Dorian, non-diatonic notes include F, G#, A#, C, and D#. Refer to Example 1 for the default chord changes. Write down a few of your ideas on the page following the *Modal Interchange Guide*. Remember, in the eternal words of Eddie Van Halen, "If it sounds right, then it is."

Navarro Music LLC

Modal Interchange Guide

Modal Interchange Options for the key of E dorian

Nate Navarro

Navarro Music LLC

Modal Interchange Practice

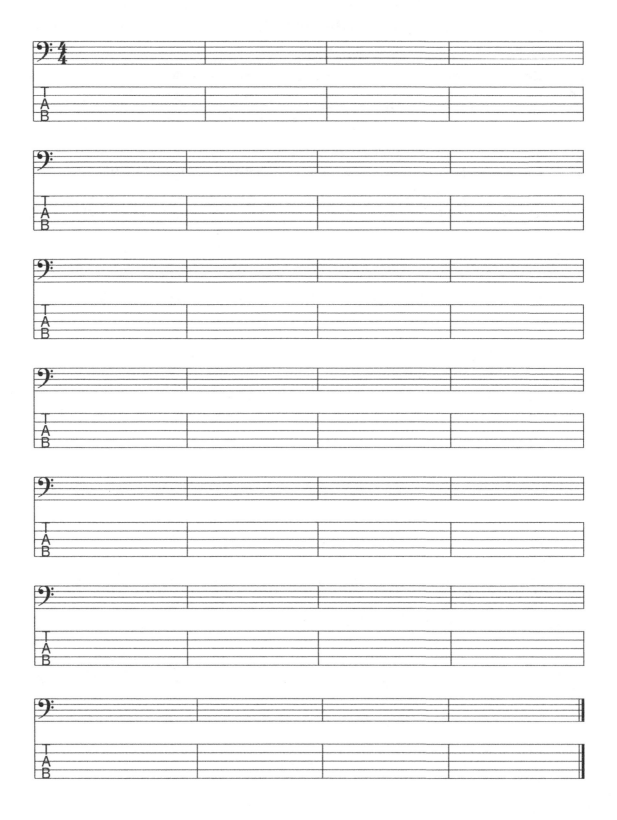

How To Write A Bass Line

Example 3: Modal Interchange

Nate Navarro ft Kris Barocsi

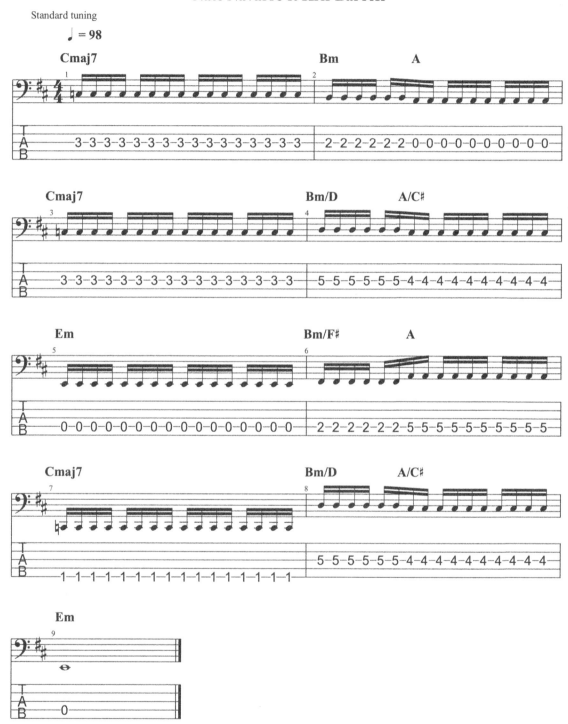

Terms to know for Example 4...

Embellishment - Non-essential notes that ornament a given passage of music.
Example: Vocal performances of national anthems at sporting events.

Example 4: Embellishment

Embellishments should act as an underscore for the main musical hooks and ideas that carry the song. Example 4 integrates embellishments through doubling key parts of Kris' guitar riff an octave lower. *Syncopation* and *Modal Interchange* are also present to give an idea of what these techniques sound like together.

It is possible, especially as the bass-role instrument, to embellish too often. Remember that our primary function in most contexts is to provide the low end (harmonically speaking), and the groove (rhythmically speaking). Use musical discernment to find just the right amount of ornamentation in spicing up that bass part to better support the overall composition.

Navarro Music LLC

Lessons -
Moderate to Advanced

How To Write A Bass Line

Example 4: Embellishment
Nate Navarro ft Kris Barocsi

Standard tuning

♩ = 98

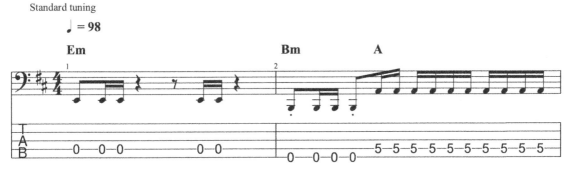

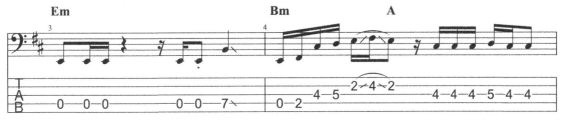

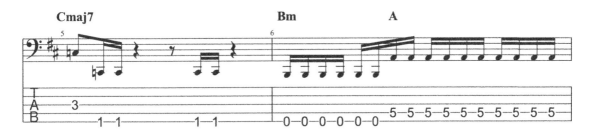

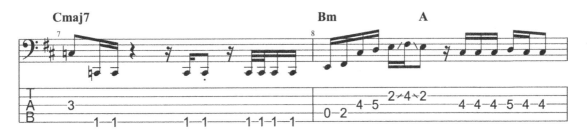

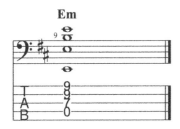

Lessons -
Moderate to Advanced

Writing Practice

When writing a bass line, listen closely to the music in order to make discerning creative decisions that will serve the piece as a whole. You might ask yourself, "are there any elements already present that I would like to emphasize?" Or, "would it be best to lay back and leave space for the other ideas already at play?" Each song or section may lend itself well to a particular creative approach, or not. For example, syncopation may serve a particular Prog Rock arrangement well, but it could be distracting in a CCM piece more suited for reharmonization. Create your own bass line for Kris' riff with these thoughts in mind, using the included bassless backing track. Write your ideas down below, and on the following page.

Writing Practice

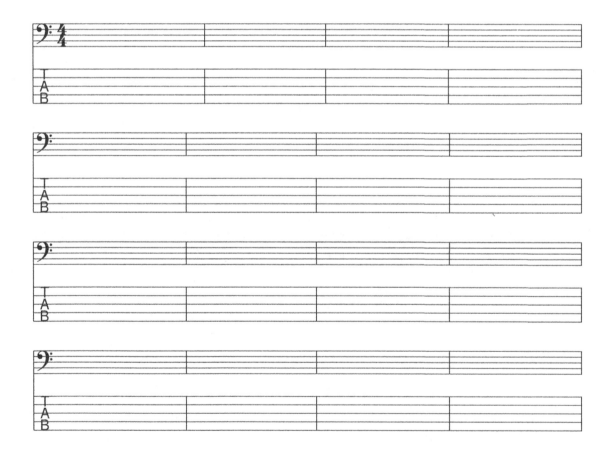

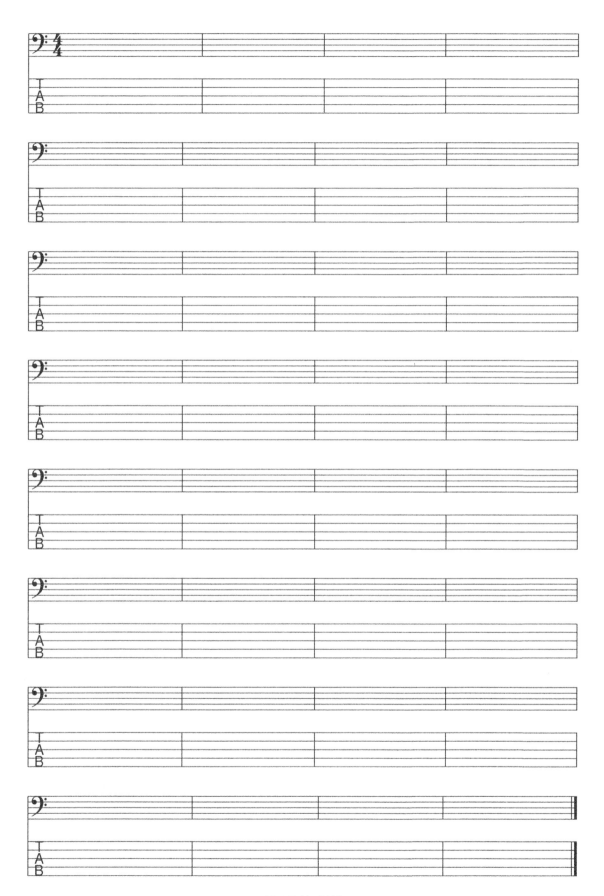

Passing Diminished Chords

Video

https://youtu.be/_CR8I6CiOOQ?t=4706

From the music of Mozart to the bass lines of James Jamerson, passing diminished chords are an effective tool in adding flavor and a sense of prowess to one's playing and progressions. In this lesson, we will learn how to use passing diminished chords, and we will also get a feel for them under our fingers, and begin recognizing them by ear. Follow along with the video linked above.

When there is a whole step between two consecutive chords in a progression, you can interpolating a passing diminished chord between them. Let's start with a three-chord progression of G Major, C Major and D Major.

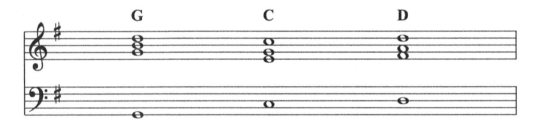

There is a whole step between the root notes of the C and D chord, which means means that we can place a C# diminished chord between them. The C# passing diminished chord builds tension, which is then resolved by the following D Major chord.

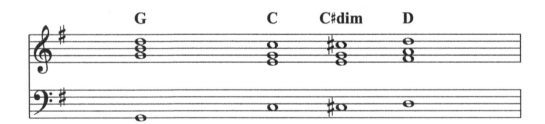

Let's cover a few exercises that will help us learn to use passing diminished chords, and since we don't usually play chords on bass, we will arpeggiate the chords instead.

For exercise 1, arpeggiate two-octave triads in the key of C Major. This will give us a better perspective of the diatonic harmony before adding in passing diminished chords.

Passing Diminished Chords
Exercise 1: Triads in C Major
Nate Navarro

For exercise 2, let's add in passing diminished chords wherever there is a distance of a whole step between two diatonic notes.

Passing Diminished Chords
Exercise 2: Triads with Passing Diminished Chords
Nate Navarro

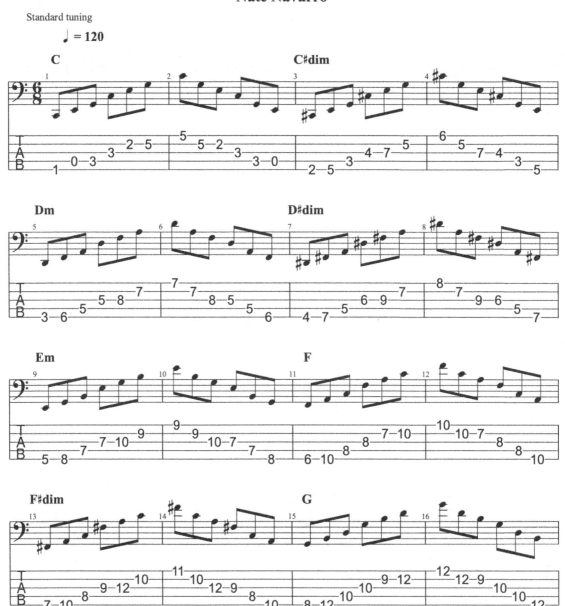

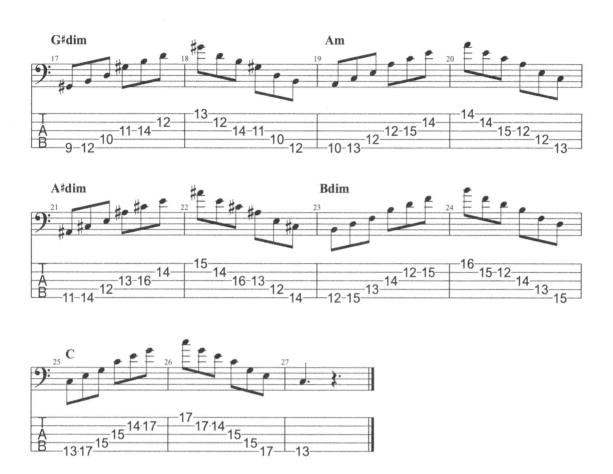

Now we're talking! I'm a fan of that slowly building evenly-spaced harmonic movement. Of course, this is just an exercise, but what do you think of the sound so far? Can you recall any music you've heard that uses passing diminished chords?

Navarro Music LLC

For exercise three, we'll go back to diatonic notes only, but instead of playing triads, we'll arpeggiate all the diatonic seventh chords within the key of C Major.

Passing Diminished Chords
Exercise 3: Diatonic Seventh Chords
Nate Navarro

*Lessons -
Moderate to Advanced*

To add a seventh to any passing diminished chord, use the diatonic note that is either a whole step, or a minor third below the root. The seventh of the passing diminished chord will always be diatonic to the key; the key will dictate whether the seventh is minor or diminished in quality, making the chord either half or fully diminished.

For example, in the key of C Major, we have a C# passing diminished chord, spelled C#, E, and G. The note B is a whole step below the root note of C#, and the note Bb is a minor third below the root note of C#. Since Bb is not diatonic to the key of C, B is the proper choice for the seventh of the C# passing diminished chord. This gives us the notes C#, E, G, and B, for a C# half diminished chord, also known as C#m7b5. This is spoken, C# minor 7 flat 5.

For another example in the key of C Major, we have a D# passing diminished chord, spelled D#, F#, A. The note C is a minor third below the root note D#, and the note C# is a whole step below the root note D#. Since C# is not diatonic to the key of C, C is the proper choice for the seventh of the D# passing diminished chord. This gives us the notes D#, F#, A, and C, for a D#°7 chord, also known as D# fully diminished.

Each of the passing diminished chords sound unique in their own context, and even more so when you add in the sevenths. Let's play all diatonic seventh chords now, and branch them together with the passing diminished seventh chords.

Passing Diminished Chords

Exercise 4: Seventh Chords with Passing Diminished Chords
Nate Navarro

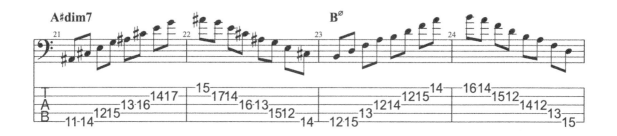

Here are a few progressions that you can use for practice in adding passing diminished chords. First, write in a passing diminished chord wherever it may fit. Remember, a passing diminished chord may be used wherever there is. a whole step between the root note of two diatonic chords. Next, arpeggiate the chord changes on your bass.

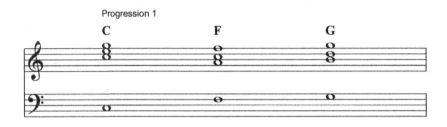

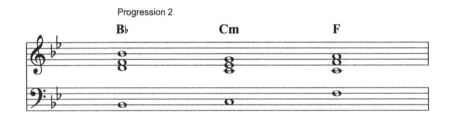

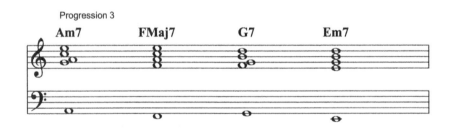

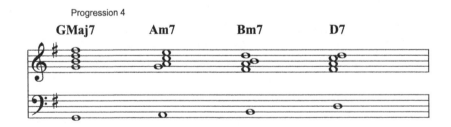

Advanced Picking Techniques

Video
https://youtu.be/_CR8I6CiOOQ?t=5239

Why learn advanced picking techniques?

In the vast majority of gigging and recording situations, the common fingerstyle or pick approach will get the job done with flying colors. However, if you find yourself wanting more speed, dexterity, and tonal options, advanced picking techniques might be for you.

In my personal experience, advanced picking techniques have enabled me to land gigs that I wouldn't have been able to otherwise, due to the technical nature of the music.
Also, in recording sessions I've had with famous producers, once they hear me play around a bit, they'll often want to experiment with the different timbres of these techniques.
"The fingerstyle take was great, now let's hear it with a pick, and then do it again with that double-thumb thing."

It's not the techniques themselves that the producers are interested in, but the tonal variation they offer. Producers always appreciate having different tones to work with, and they'll remember you for that.

Lessons -
Moderate to Advanced

Three-Finger-Picking (Ring, Middle, Index)

Video 🎥
https://youtu.be/_CR8I6CiOOQ?t=5302

Your ring finger is similar in length to your index finger; angle your hand so that the ring and index finger have roughly the same angle of attack on the strings. Bend your middle finger so that it strikes the strings in line with other fingers. Pluck in this order: Ring, Middle, Index, and then repeat.

Let's begin with a sole focus on the ring finger. We will not pluck with any other fingers for Exercise 1. Play along with me, using the video linked at the beginning of this section.

Lessons -
Moderate to Advanced

You might notice that picking with your ring finger sounds different than picking with your other fingers, and there are a number of factors causing this: each finger has a different texture; your ring finger is likely less calloused, than the other two. They also have different surface areas coming into contact with the string, due to their varying thickness. Add to this, unequal lengths and strengths, and the slightly different points at which they strike the strings, and there is a discernible difference in their sound.

As you practice, your ring finger will get stronger, and more calloused, and this *will* help improve the uniformity of your picking, but it will never sound perfectly alike, and this is actually a good thing. Details such as these make performances sound alive, rather than having the energy of a stale MIDI render. That said, still attempt to create an equal sound between your fingers, as much as you can. This will exercise dynamic control, which is fundamental to emotive playing.

When musically fitting, you may choose to add compression and perhaps overdrive or distortion to your bass signal. These effects can aid in evening the dynamics of each finger while increasing tonal uniformity. At the end of the day, your fingers are awesomely human. They are not MIDI. Let us embrace our human "imperfections."

Now let's play Exercise 2. This time we will use all three fingers. As we descend the strings, use right-hand raking. The right-hand fingerings are written out for the entire exercise.

Advanced Picking Techniques
Three Finger Picking Ex 2
Nate Navarro

Standard tuning

♩ = 70

When practicing a new technique, it is often helpful to play a bass line that you're already familiar with, perhaps on the simpler side, and instead of playing it your usual way, use the new technique. Let's play Beginner Example 1 "Latin Blues," using three fingers.

Advanced Picking Techniques
Three Finger Picking Ex 3
Nate Navarro

Practice Continued - *Three Finger Picking*

Take time to become acquainted with three finger picking. Follow these steps at your own pace for further practice.

Practice 1
Play through all of the Finger Independence exercises using only your ring finger to pluck. Focus on getting a consistent sound and accurate timing for each pluck. Play along with the video lessons, or use a metronome if you like. Having a constant beat to play to will be helpful.

Practice 2
Play through all of the Finger Independence exercises using the three finger picking technique. Incorporate raking when descending strings, and focus on equal tone between fingers and accurate timing. Play along with the video lessons, or use a metronome.

Practice 3
Play bass lines that you are already familiar with, but use the three finger picking technique.

Navarro Music LLC

Lessons -
Moderate to Advanced

Four-Finger Picking (Pinky-Ring-Middle-Index)

Video
https://youtu.be/_CR8I6CiOOQ?t=5575

Four-finger picking is useful in playing fast lines, adding in quick, flam-like embellishments, and it pairs well with double bass drum beats. Some players have told me that this technique is *impossible* for them, due to their pinky being too short; until I show them *this trick...*

On the G-string, play frets 17, 18, 19, and 20. As you do, keep each finger held down against the frets.

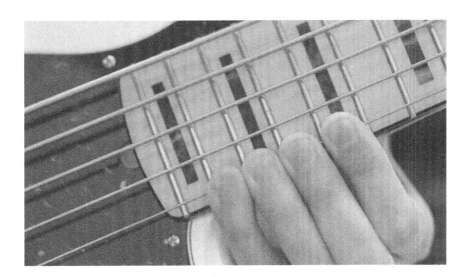

See how they all line up in a row, with the fleshy part of each finger contacting the string? We need to use this same approach with four finger picking. Keeping your fretting hand fingers where they are, and line up your picking-hand fingertips with them.

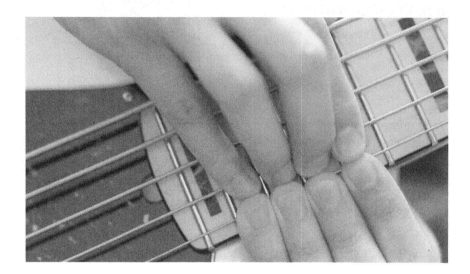

We now have all of our plucking-hand fingers in the right form, so let's just slide them towards the pickups, and now they're in the right position.

Stay here on the D string, and play open-string 8th notes plucking with our pinky, index, middle, and ring, then repeating. Remember to keep all of the other strings muted using right-hand muting and the close fretting method. Follow along with the video.

Advanced Picking Techniques
Four Finger Picking (PRMI) Ex 1
Nate Navarro

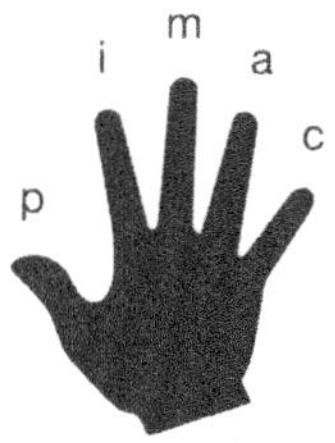

Standard tuning

♩ = 70

Similar to three finger picking, you'll notice that your pinky has a unique sound. Your four finger picking will become more uniform with practice, but none of your fingers will ever sound identical. Again, that's a good thing.

Let's play Beginner Example 2: Gojishuggah, using four-finger picking.

Advanced Picking Techniques
Four Finger Picking (PRMI) Ex 2
Nate Navarro

Practice Continued - *Four Finger Picking (Pinky, Ring, Middle, Index)*

Take time to become acquainted with four finger picking (PRMI). Follow these steps at your own pace for further practice.

Practice 1
Play through all of the Finger Independence exercises using only your **pinky** finger to pluck. Focus on getting a consistent sound and accurate timing . Play along with the video lessons, or use a metronome if you like. Having a constant beat to play to will be helpful.

Practice 2
Repeat ALL of the Finger Independence exercises using only your **ring** finger to pluck. Again, focus on getting a consistent sound and accurate timing. Play along with the video lessons, or use a metronome.

Practice 3
Practice all of the Finger Independence exercises using both your ring and pinky fingers, alternating between the two of them, just as you would with the usual index and middle finger fingerstyle technique. The same focus applies: a consistent sound *(between the two fingers now)* and accurate timing. Also keep in mind the unchangeable tonal factors, mentioned earlier.

Practice 4
Play through all of the Finger Independence exercises using the four finger picking (PRMI) technique. Incorporate raking when descending strings, and focus on equal tone between fingers and accurate timing. Play along with the video lessons, or use a metronome.

Practice 5
Play bass lines that you are already familiar with, but use the four finger picking (PMRI) technique.

Practice 6
Learn Moderate to Advanced Riffs & Etudes...
      Example 17: 4-Finger Pickup
      Example 18: Raking & 4-Fingers
      Example 19: 4-Finger Blues
      Example 20: Fingerstyle Runs
      Example 30: Slap Adding 4-Finger

Four-Finger Picking (Thumb-Index-Middle-Ring)

Video 🎥
https://youtu.be/_CR8I6CiOOQ?t=5738

The Thumb-Index-Middle-Ring Four-Finger approach is a good fit for bass lines requiring more speed and less intensity in the attack, such as certain styles within fusion and jazz. This technique also works well for chordal playing.

The correct posture for this technique is more intuitive. Rest the pad of your thumb on the A string and keep your fingers curled beneath the A string without touching it. The thumb will pluck the A string in a downward motion, and then the index, middle, and ring fingers will each pluck the string upwardly.

Let's move to the D string now, and play open eighth notes together. Follow along with the video.

Advanced Picking Techniques
Four Finger Picking (TIRM) Ex 1
Nate Navarro

Now let's add in all the strings and left-hand fretting, with a two-octave CMaj7 arpeggio, starting on the first fret of the B-string. We'll play each note four times.

Advanced Picking Techniques
Four Finger Picking (TIRM) Ex 2
Nate Navarro

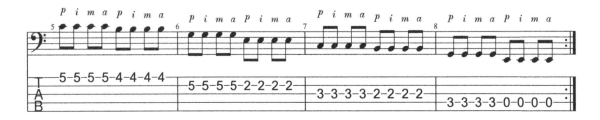

Lessons -
Moderate to Advanced

Practice Continued - *Four Finger Picking (Thumb, Index, Middle Ring)*

Take time to become acquainted with four finger picking (TIMR). Follow these steps at your own pace for further practice.

Practice 1
Play through all of the Finger Independence exercises using the four finger picking (TIMR) technique. Focus on equal tone between fingers and accurate timing. Play along with the video lessons, or use a metronome.

Practice 2
Play bass lines that you are already familiar with, but use the four finger picking (TIMR) technique.

Practice 3
Learn Moderate to Advanced Riffs & Etudes...
>   Example 12: Thumb Pluck
>   Example 13: Arpeggiated Chords
>   Example 14: Chordal Etude
>   Example 21: Adding Slap

Double Thumb

Video

https://youtu.be/_CR8I6CiOOQ?t=5857

Applications of the Double Thumb technique are wide-ranging. I tend to use it most when the music calls for an aggressive attack and a cleaner tone; often in metal, rock, and funk. For different tones, the thumb can strike the string at different points - closer to and farther from the bridge. I prefer the thickness in sound I get when striking at the highest frets on the neck. In this position, the fingerboard serves as a ramp for my thumb; keeping the depth of my thumb about the same on both the down-swing and the up-swing.

For the Double Thumb technique, the thumb is essentially mimicking a pick, more than it is using a modified version of slap. When holding a pick, the angle of your thumb relative to the string floats around 20 to 40 degrees. This range is effective in Double Thumb as well. On the down-swing, the thumb strikes the string against the frets. On the up-swing the thumb strinkes the string with the hard surface of the thumbnail, for a similar timbre. Practice using the same intensity in both directions for a more even sound.

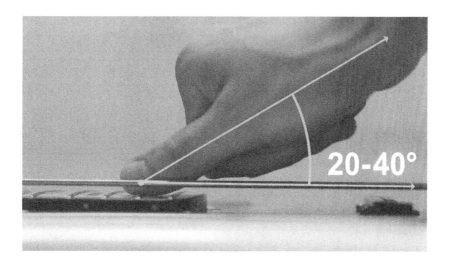

Let's play eighth notes on the fifth fret of the E string. Remember to use the "close fretting method" covered in the *Intro to Fingerstyle* section. Play along and see in-depth demonstrations of the Double Thumb technique in the video linked at the beginning of this section.

Advanced Picking Techniques
Double Thumb Ex 1
Nate Navarro

Advanced Picking Techniques
Double Thumb Ex 2
Nate Navarro

Navarro Music LLC

Advanced Picking Techniques
Double Thumb Ex 3
Nate Navarro

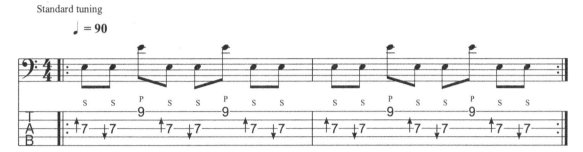

Practice Continued - *Double Thumb*

Take time to become acquainted with the Double Thumb technique. Follow these steps at your own pace for further practice.

Practice 1
Practice all of the *Finger Independence* exercises while using the Double Thumb technique. Attempt to keep an even tone and accurate timing.

Practice 2
Play bass lines that you are already familiar with, but use the Double Thumb technique.

Practice 3
Learn Moderate to Advanced Riffs & Etudes...
    Example 26: Adding Double Thumb
    Example 27: Slap & Strum
    Example 28: Flam Pop
    Example 29: Double Thumb Burst
    Example 30: Slap adding 4-Finger
    Example 31: Slap, Tap, 4-Finger
    Example 32: Pickup Tapping
    Example 38: Thumb Bleed

Sweep Picking

Video 🎥

https://youtu.be/_CR8I6CiOOQ?t=6073

Here's a good way to get fired... or hired, depending on the context.
Let's give 'em the old razzle-dazzle with a D Major arpeggio, starting on the 10th fret of the E string. Follow along with the video linked above.

Sweep Picking Step 1: Remember the reverse portion of the Double Thumb technique that we covered in the last section? Use the up-swing of the thumb to play the first note.

Sweep Picking Step 2: Hammer-on the 14th fret of the E string.

Sweep Picking Step 3: Use your thumb to sweep across the A, D, and G strings - frets 12, 12, and 11, respectively. Fret the A and D string by bridging your middle finger across both strings.

Sweep Picking Step 4: Hammer-on the 14th fret of the G string.

Sweep Picking Step 5: Tap the 19th fret of the G string with your right hand.

Lessons -
Moderate to Advanced

Let's loop these steps and play them together in Sweep Picking Example 1.

Advanced Picking Techniques
Sweep Picking Ex 1
Nate Navarro

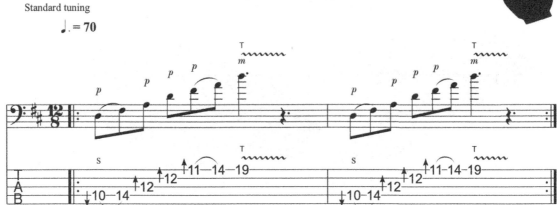

Now, picking up at Step 6 for the descent...

Sweep Picking Step 6: From the tap on the 19th fret, pull-off to frets 14 and 11 of the G string.

Sweep Picking Step 7: Use your index finger to rake/sweep down the D, A, and E strings, frets 12, 12, and 14 respectively. Fret the D and A string by bridging your middle finger across both strings.

Sweep Picking Step 8: Use your middle finger to pluck the last note of the arpeggio on the E string, back at the 10th fret in this case.

Let's practice just the descent now, as Sweep Picking Example 2.

Navarro Music LLC

Use a combination of both left-hand and right-hand muting to keep the sweep sounding clean. Let's play the ascent and descent together.

Practice Continued - *Sweep Picking*

Take time to become acquainted with Sweep Picking. Follow these steps at your own pace for further practice.

Practice 1
Practice two-octave Major triads all over the neck...

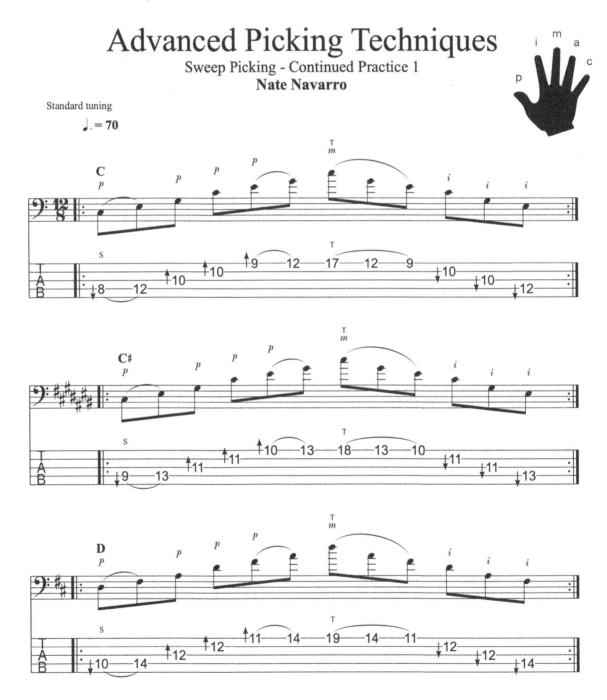

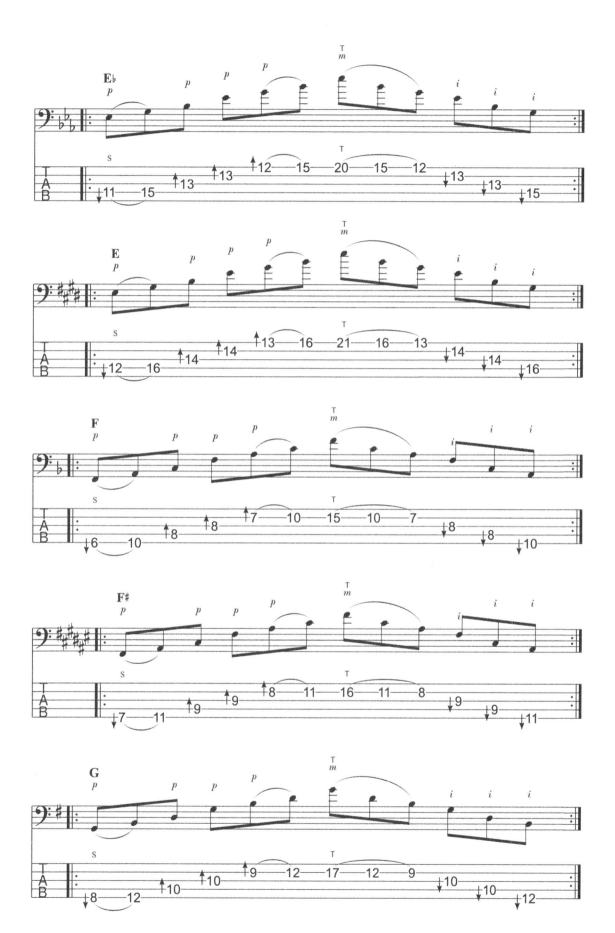

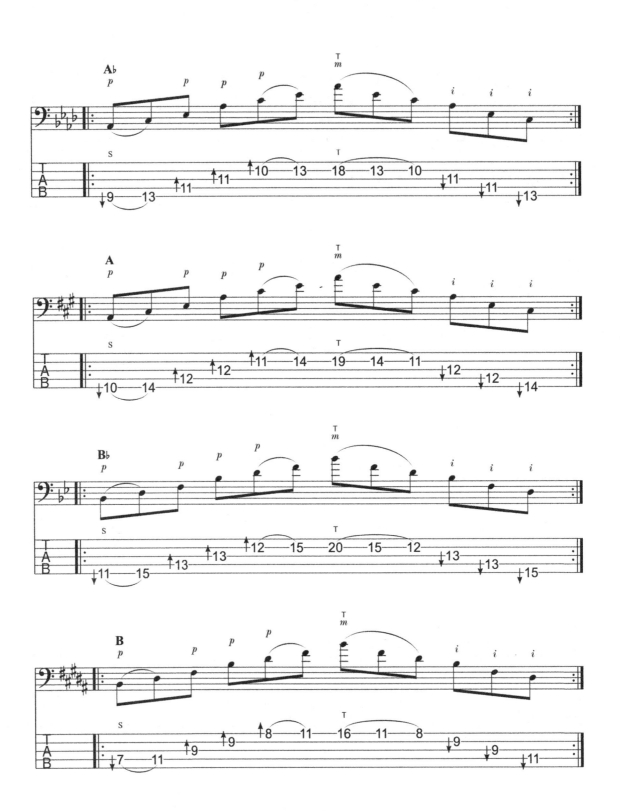

Practice 2

Practice C minor, C Augmented, and C diminished arpeggios.

C minor - fret the A and D strings with your bridged ring finger.

C Augmented - fret the A string with your ring finger and fret the D string with your middle finger.

C diminished - fret the A string with your middle finger and fret the D string with your ring finger.

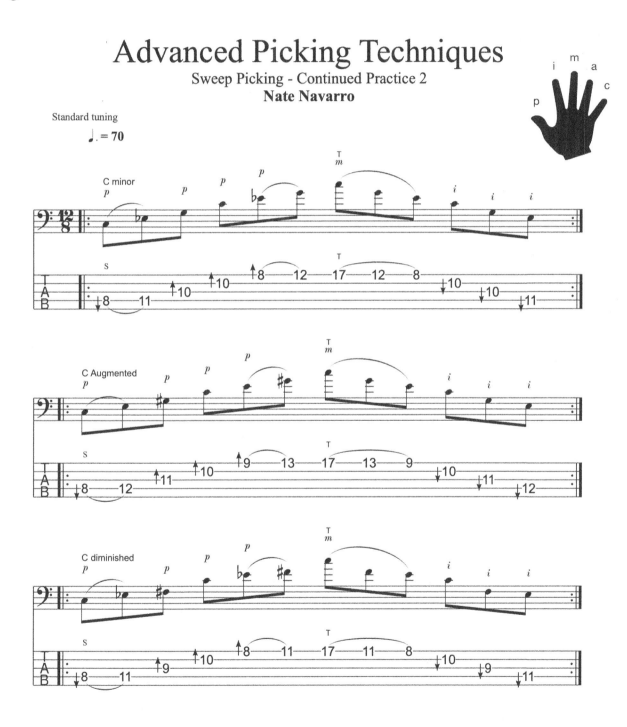

Practice 3

Memorize the fretting-hand shapes of Major, minor, Augmented, and diminished arpeggios. Practice them across the neck.

Practice 4

Learn Moderate to Advanced Riffs & Etudes...

        Example 55: Horizon

        Example 56: Element

        Example 60: Interdimensional War

Riffs & Etudes - Moderate to Advanced

Video

https://youtu.be/_CR8I6CiOOQ?t=6296

Rhythmic Shift
Example 1
Nate Navarro

Soft VS Loud

Example 2
Nate Navarro

Navarro Music LLC

The "Shake"
Example 3
Nate Navarro

Navarro Music LLC

Hammers & Slides
Example 4
Nate Navarro

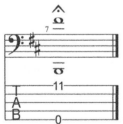

Navarro Music LLC

Adding Harmonics
Example 5
Nate Navarro

Standard tuning

♩ = 105

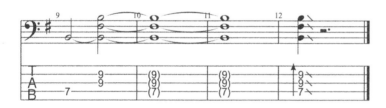

Navarro Music LLC

Bouncy Muted Notes

Example 6
Nate Navarro

Syncopated Mutes

Example 7
Nate Navarro

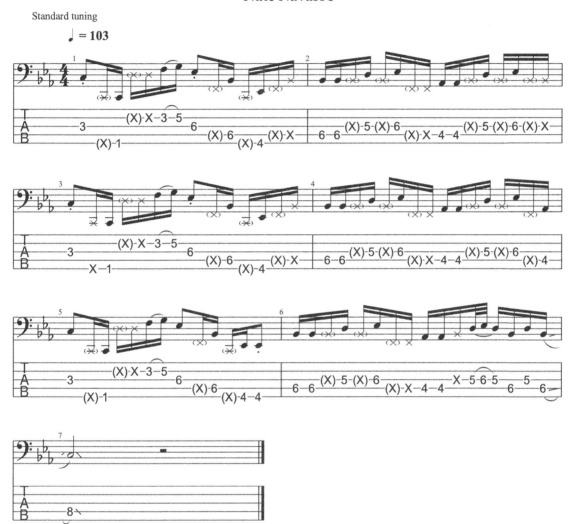

Navarro Music LLC

Fingerstyle Swing
Example 8
Nate Navarro

Riffs & Etudes -
Moderate to Advanced

String Crossing
Example 9
Nate Navarro

Standard tuning

♩ = 100

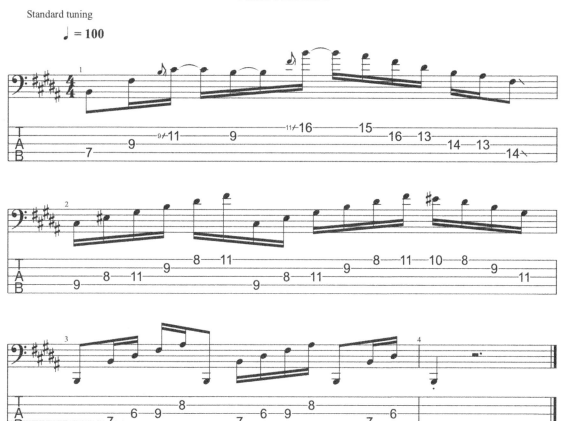

Triple Rock Etude
Example 10
Nate Navarro

Modern Jazz Etude

Example 11
Nate Navarro

Navarro Music LLC
All rights reserved - International Copyright Secured

Thumb Pluck
Example 12
Nate Navarro

Standard tuning

♩ = 116

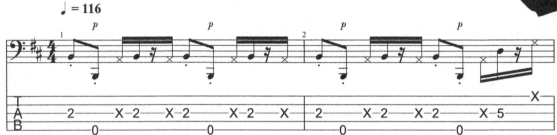

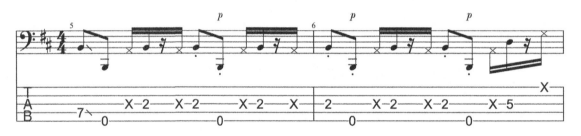

Riffs & Etudes -
Moderate to Advanced

Navarro Music LLC

116

Arpeggiating Chords
Example 13
Nate Navarro

Standard tuning

♩ = 79

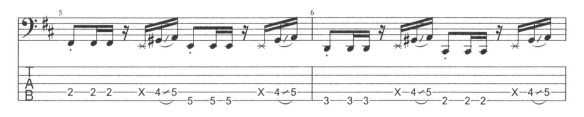

Chordal Etude
Example 14
Nate Navarro

Fingerstyle & Harmonics Groove
Example 15
Nate Navarro

Standard tuning

♩ = 105

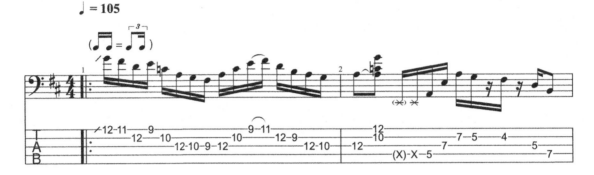

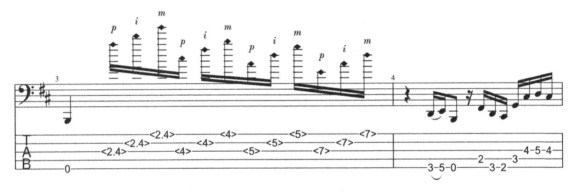

Adding Strumming

Example 16
Nate Navarro

Tune down 1 step
①= F ③= G ⑤= A
②= C ④= D

♩ = 140

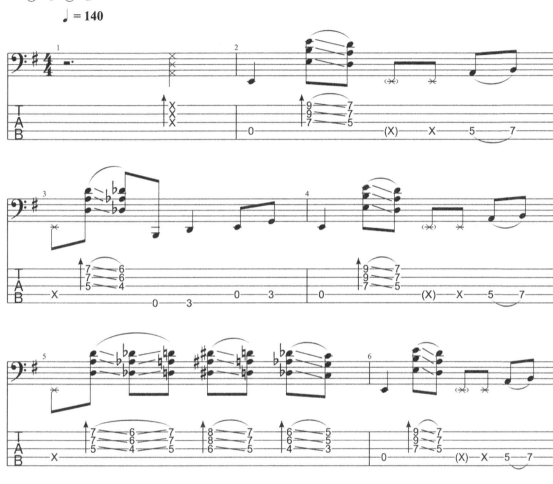

Riffs & Etudes -
Moderate to Advanced

Navarro Music LLC

Navarro Music LLC

4-Finger Pickup
Example 17
Nate Navarro

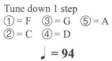

Tune down 1 step
① = F ③ = G ⑤ = A
② = C ④ = D

♩ = 94

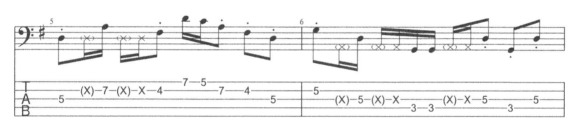

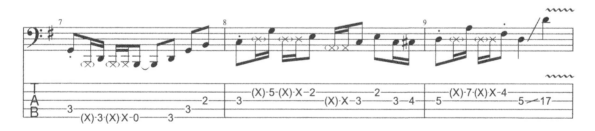

Raking & 4-Fingers
Example 18
Nate Navarro

4-Finger Blues
Example 19
Nate Navarro

Fingerstyle Runs
Example 20
Nate Navarro

Standard tuning

♩ = 115

Riffs & Etudes -
Moderate to Advanced

Navarro Music LLC

126

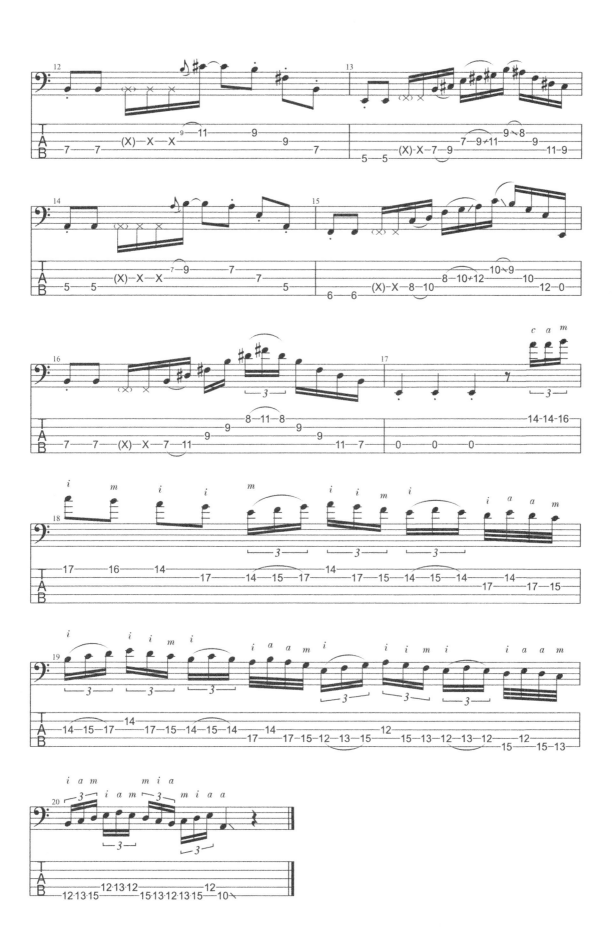

Adding Slap
Example 21
Nate Navarro

Mixed Fingerstyle & Slap
Example 22
Nate Navarro

Swung 16th's Slapped
Example 23
Nate Navarro

Slap & Harmonics Groove

Example 24
Nate Navarro

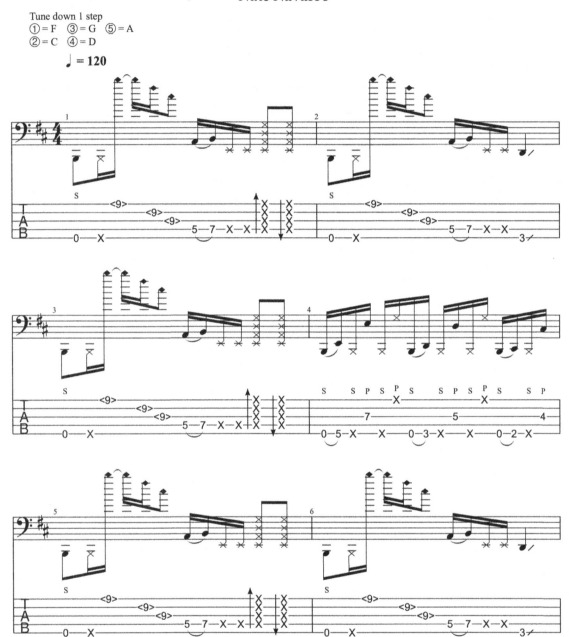

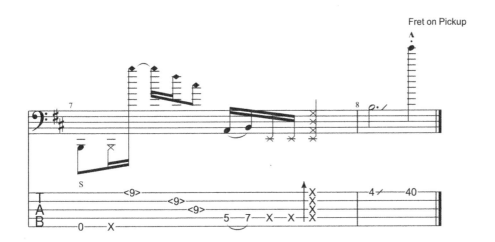

Navarro Music LLC

Slap & Chords
Example 25
Nate Navarro

Navarro Music LLC

*Riffs & Etudes -
Moderate to Advanced*

Adding Double Thumb

Example 26
Nate Navarro

Navarro Music LLC

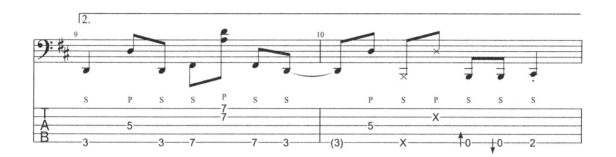

Slap & Strum
Example 27
Nate Navarro

Navarro Music LLC

Flam Pop
Example 28
Nate Navarro

Standard tuning

$\quad$ = 142

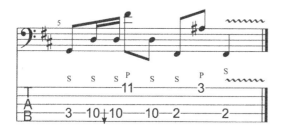

Navarro Music LLC
All rights reserved · International Copyright Secured

Double Thumb Burst

Example 29
Nate Navarro

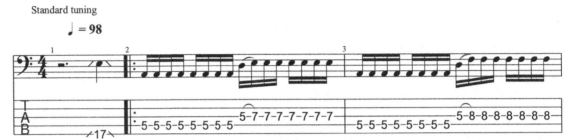

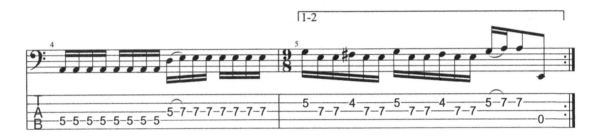

Navarro Music LLC

Slap Adding 4-Finger
Example 30
Nate Navarro

Slap, Tap, 4-Finger

Example 31
Nate Navarro

Pickup Tapping
Example 32
Nate Navarro

Standard tuning

♩ = 101

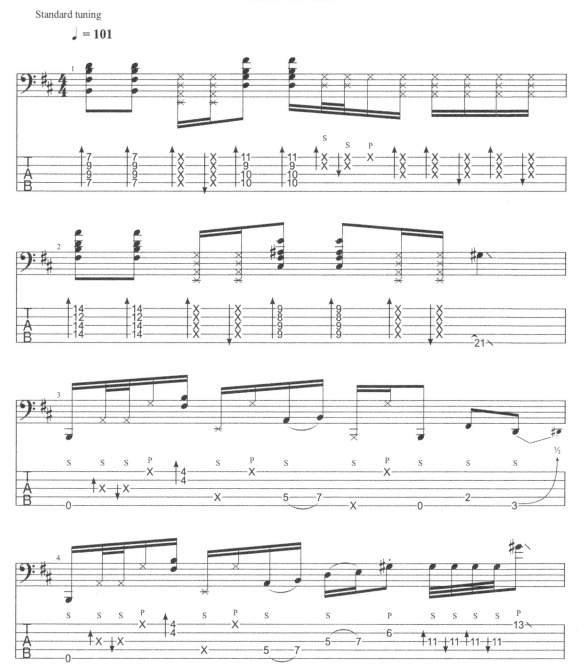

Riffs & Etudes -
Moderate to Advanced

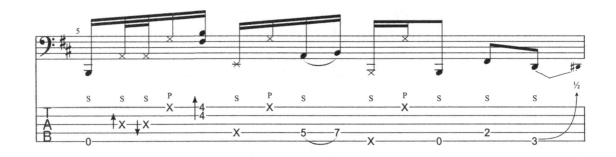

(Tap String Against Pickups)

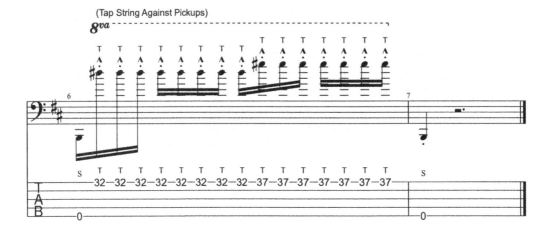

Navarro Music LLC

Mixed Tech Groove

Example 33

Nate Navarro

Navarro Music LLC

Mixed Tech Groove 2

Example 34

Nate Navarro

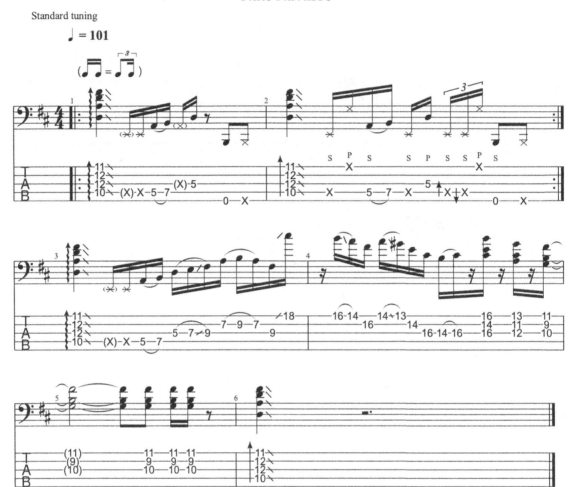

Mixed Tech Bass Line

Example 35
Nate Navarro

Mixed Tech Bass Line 2

Example 36
Nate Navarro

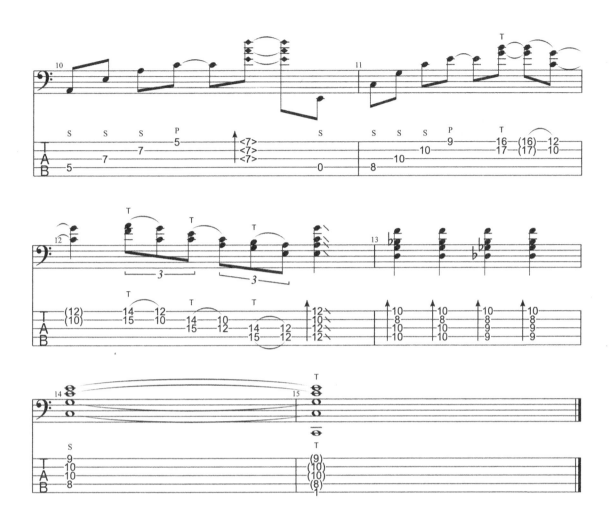

Flam Strum
Example 37
Nate Navarro

Thumb Bleed

Example 38
Nate Navarro

Navarro Music LLC

Navarro Music LLC

Dirt Road Pickin'

Example 39
Nate Navarro

Down Picking

Example 40
Nate Navarro

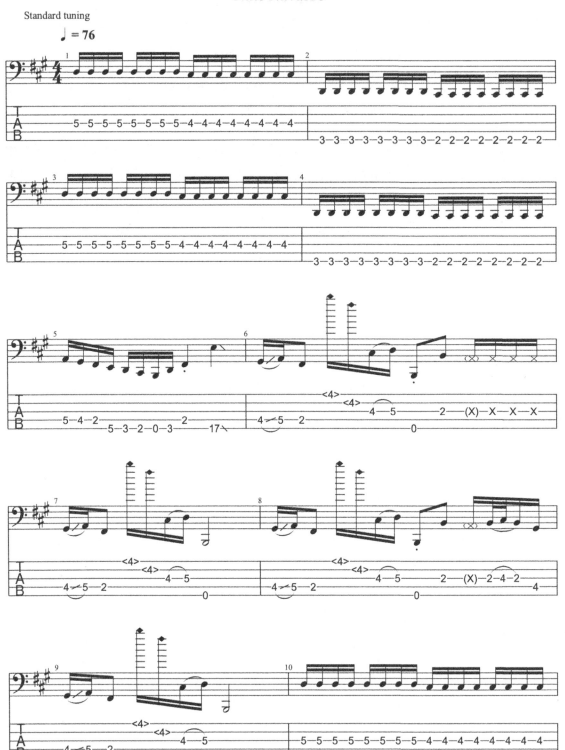

Navarro Music LLC

Riffs & Etudes -
Moderate to Advanced

Pick & Power Chords
Example 41
Nate Navarro

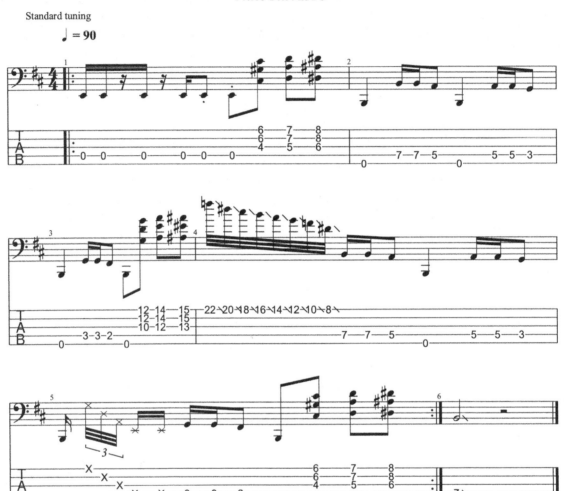

Alegro Picking
Example 42
Nate Navarro

Navarro Music LLC

Presto Picking
Example 43
Nate Navarro

Navarro Music LLC

Picking Harmonics
Example 44
Nate Navarro

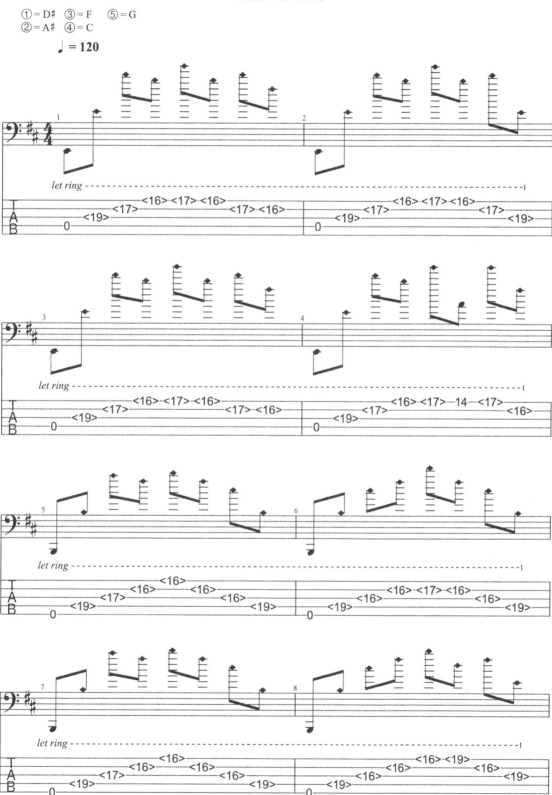

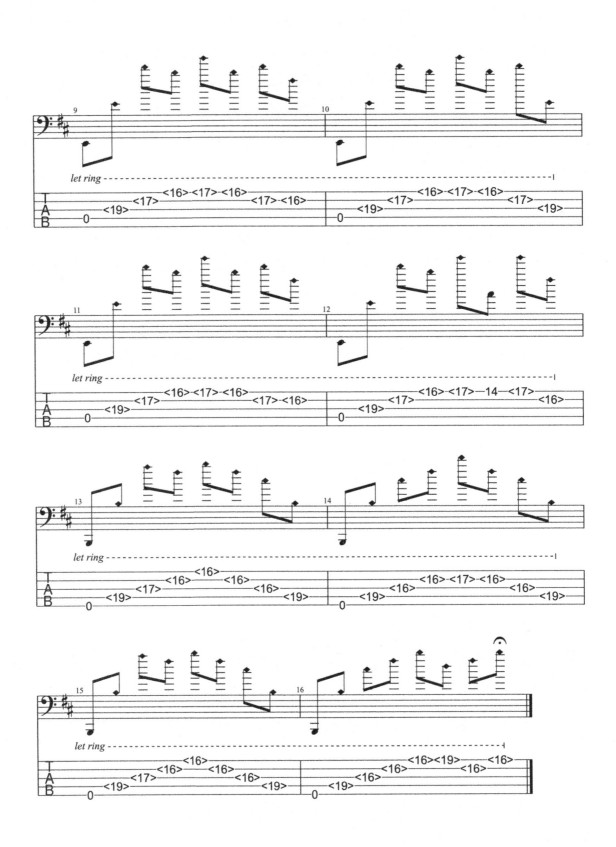

Navarro Music LLC

Mixed Meter Picking

Example 45
Nate Navarro

Navarro Music LLC
All rights reserved - International Copyright Secured

Burst Picking
Example 46
Nate Navarro

Riffs & Etudes -
Moderate to Advanced

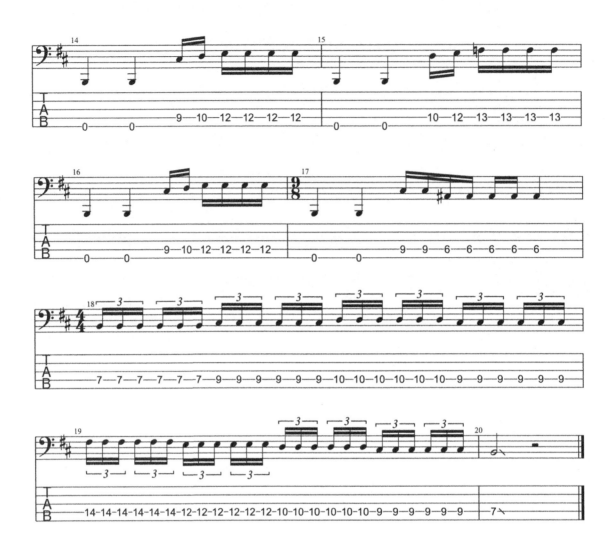

Navarro Music LLC
All rights reserved - International Copyright Secured

Picking Chromatic Runs

Example 47
Nate Navarro

Palm Mute Picking
Example 48
Nate Navarro

Riffs & Etudes -
Moderate to Advanced

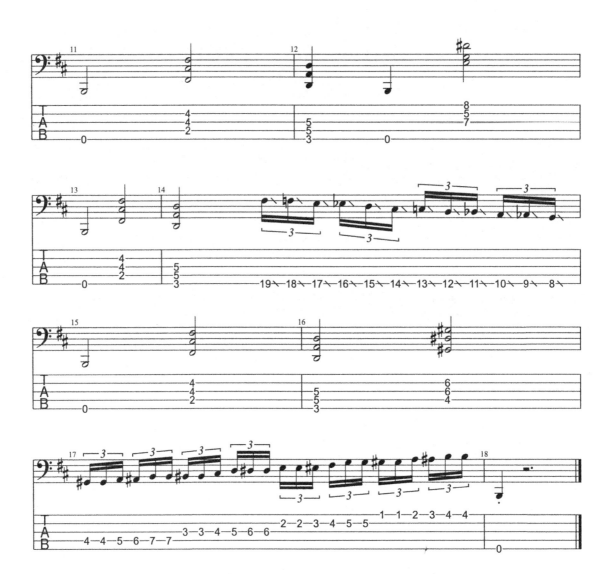

Navarro Music LLC

Fuse
Example 49
Nate Navarro

Tune down 1 step
① = F ③ = G ⑤ = A
② = C ④ = D

♩ = 100

Navarro Music LLC
All rights reserved - International Copyright Secured

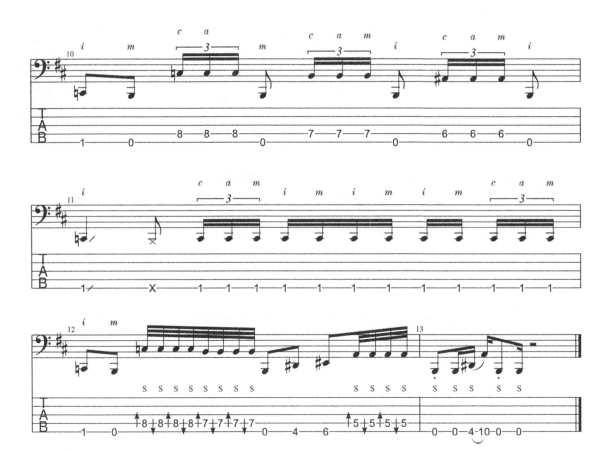

Chase

Example 50

Nate Navarro

Navarro Music LLC

Gnash
Example 51
Nate Navarro

Navarro Music LLC

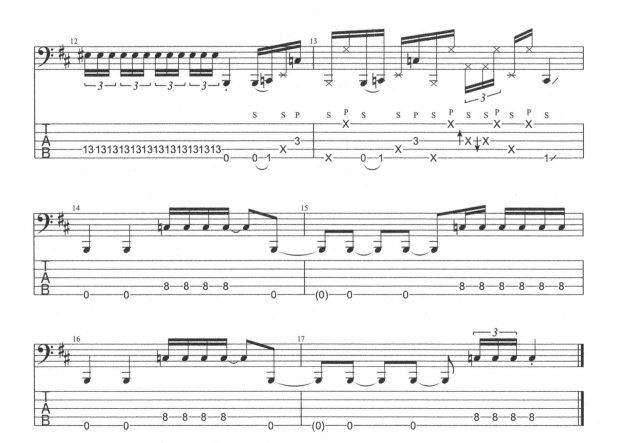

Neural
Example 52
Nate Navarro

Navarro Music LLC

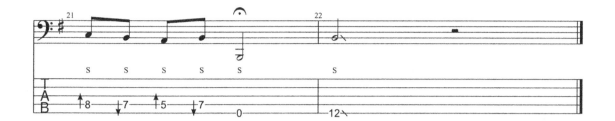

Ascension

Example 53
Nate Navarro

Standard tuning

♩ = 160

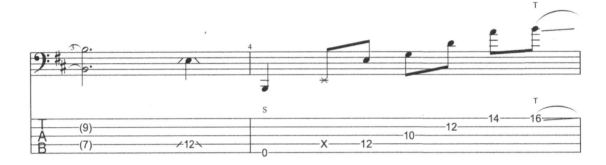

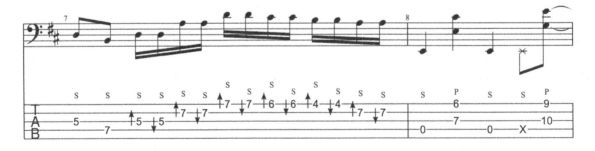

Navarro Music LLC
All rights reserved - International Copyright Secured

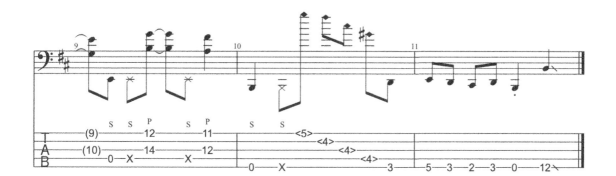

Tides
Example 54
Nate Navarro

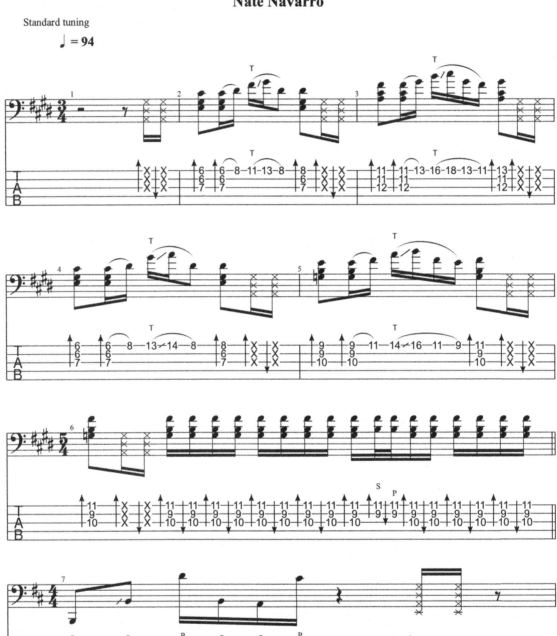

Standard tuning

♩ = 94

Riffs & Etudes -
Moderate to Advanced

Riffs & Etudes -
Moderate to Advanced

Horizon
Example 55
Nate Navarro

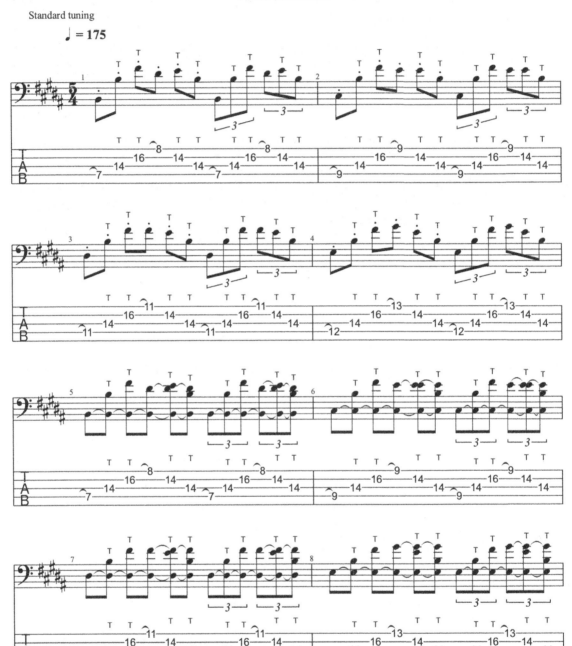

Navarro Music LLC

Navarro Music LLC

Element

Example 56
Nate Navarro

Standard tuning

♩ = 130

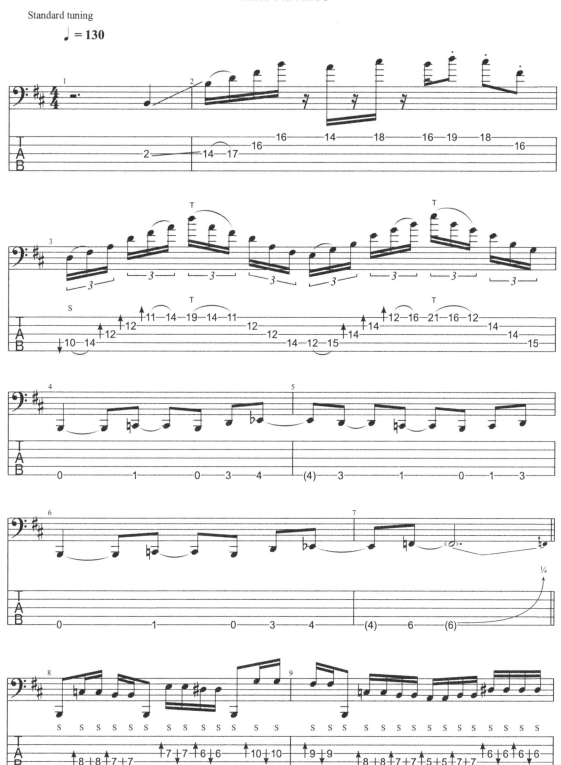

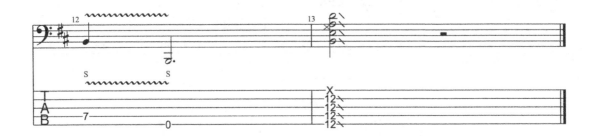

Navarro Music LLC

N Squared

Example 57
Nate Navarro

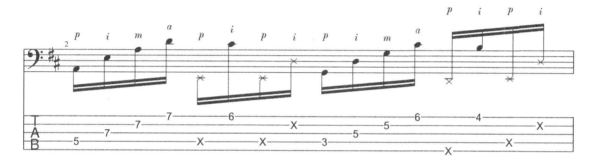

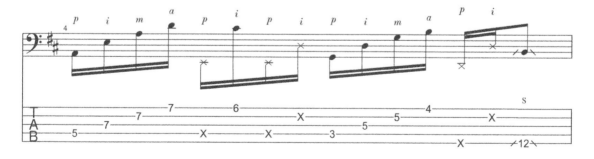

Navarro Music LLC

Navarro Music LLC

Oblivion
Example 58
Nate Navarro

Navarro Music LLC

Cliffs of Titan
Example 59
Nate Navarro

Standard tuning

♩ = 110

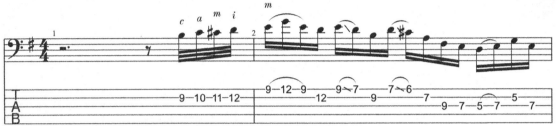

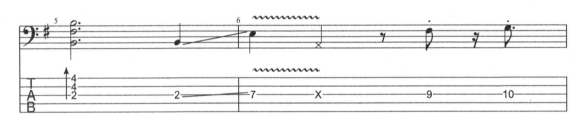

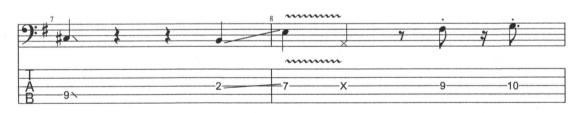

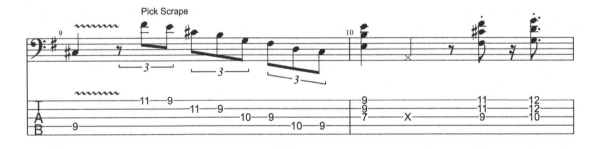

Riffs & Etudes -
Moderate to Advanced

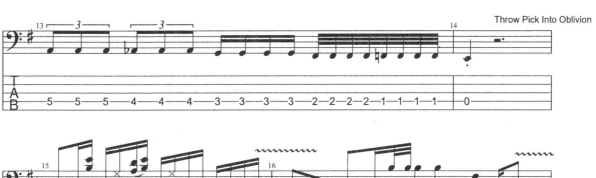

Throw Pick Into Oblivion

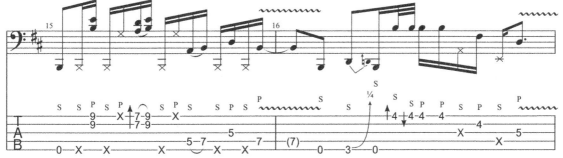

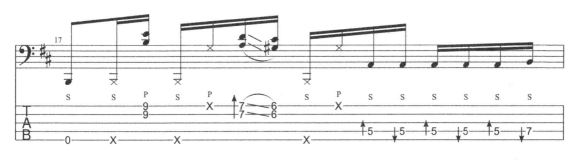

Navarro Music LLC

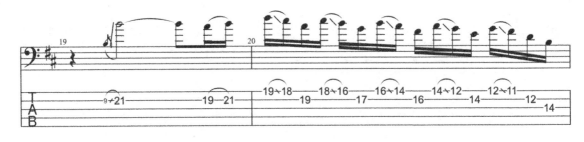

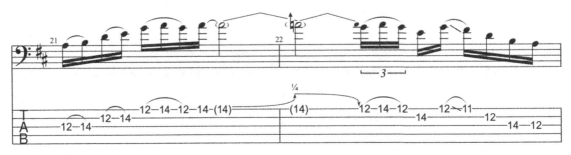

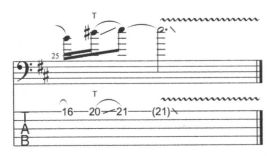

Navarro Music LLC

Interdimensional War

Example 60

Nate Navarro

Throw Pick Into Oblivion

Navarro Music LLC

Lacrimosa

Video

https://youtu.be/_CR8I6CiOOQ?t=8144

Lacrimosa
Arranged for Solo Bass by Nate Navarro
Wolfgang Amadeus Mozart

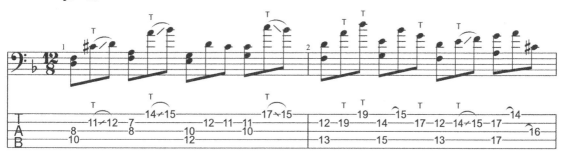

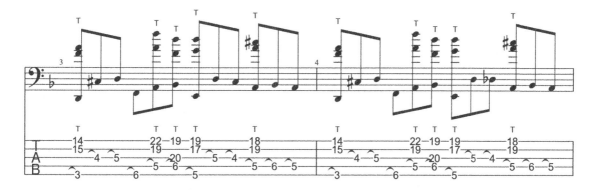

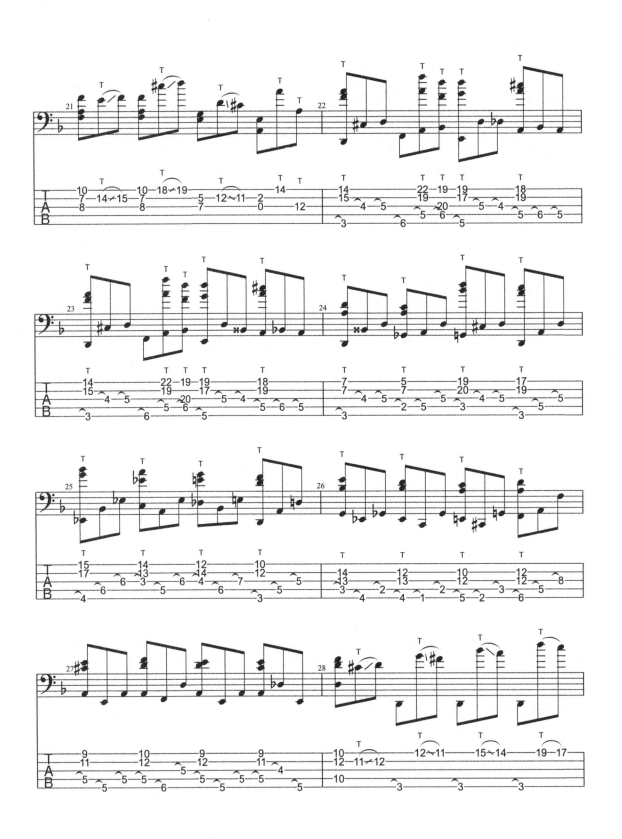

Navarro Music LLC

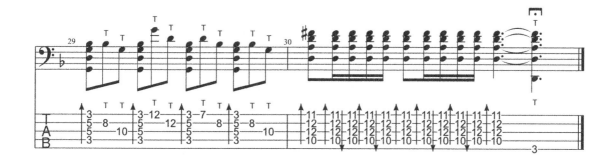

Symmetry

Symmetry
Nate Navarro

(Beat 1: Fingernails ↓, thumb ↓, thumbnail ↑, index finger ↑, fingernails ↓)

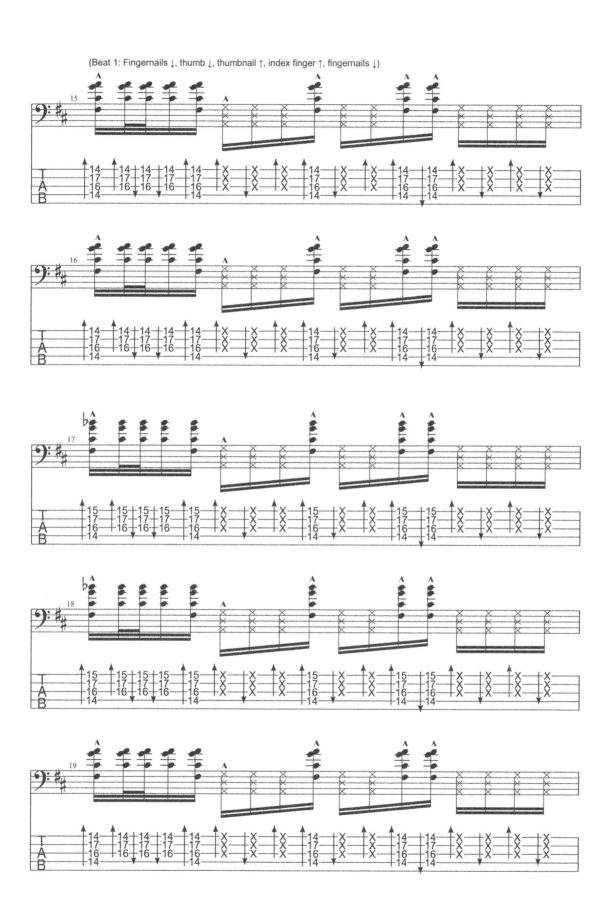

Navarro Music LLC

Navarro Music LLC

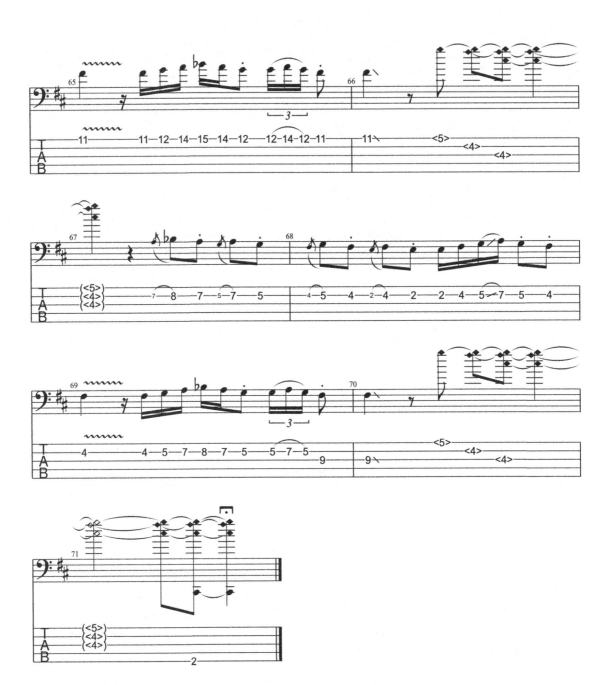

Mr. Green Eyes

Video

https://youtu.be/_CR8I6CiOOQ?t=8479

Mr. Green Eyes
Nate Navarro & Dylan Laine

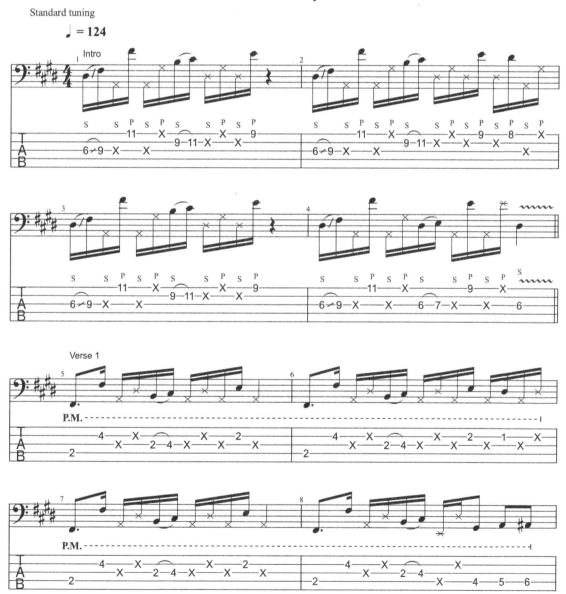

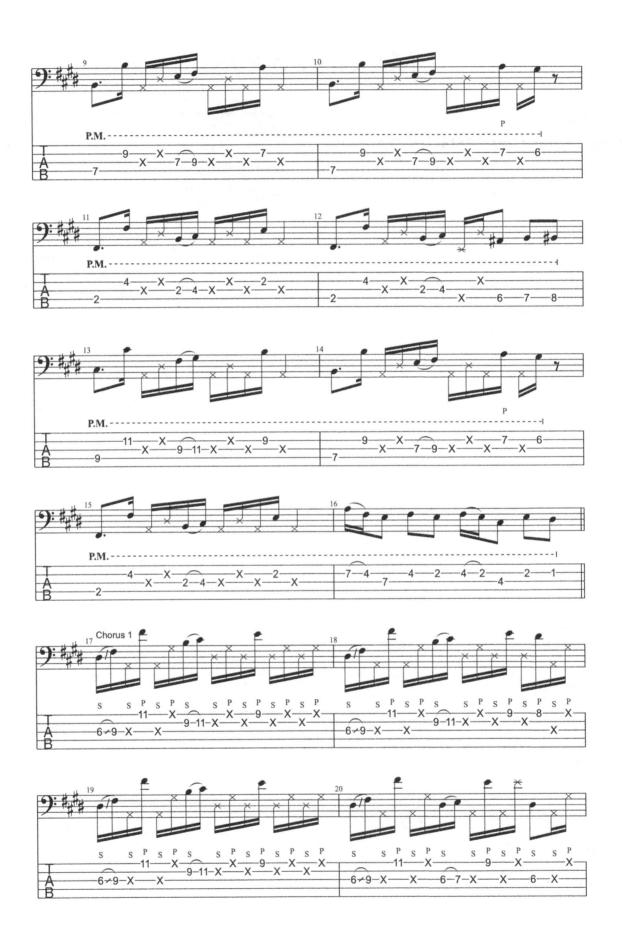

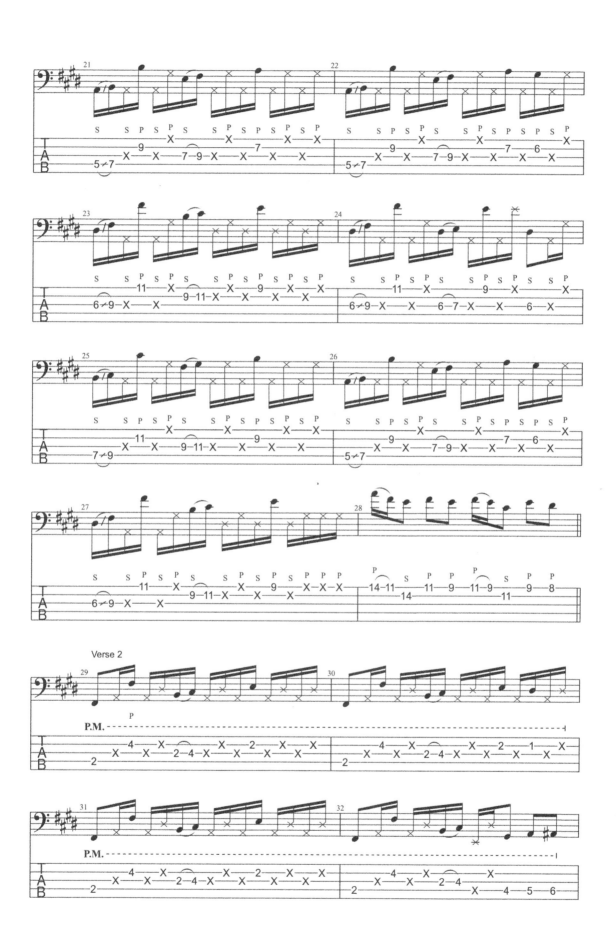

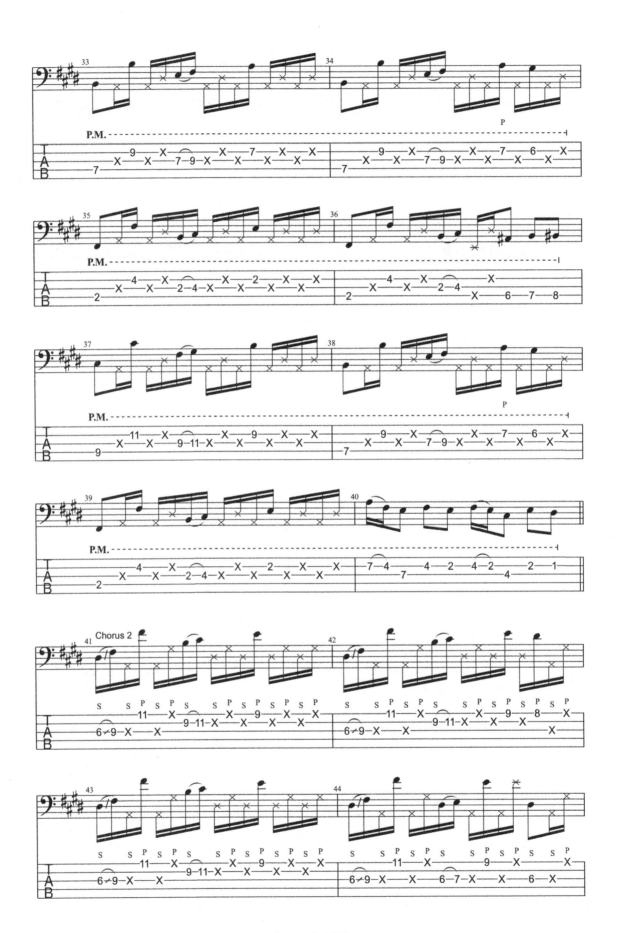

Navarro Music LLC
All rights reserved - International Copyright Secured

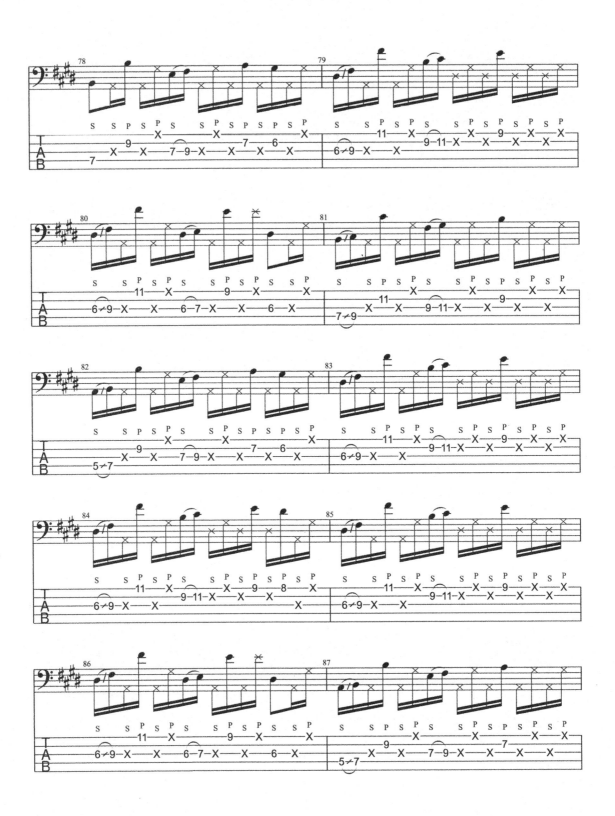

Navarro Music LLC

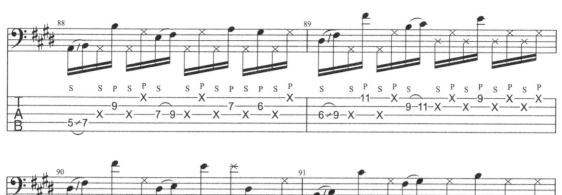

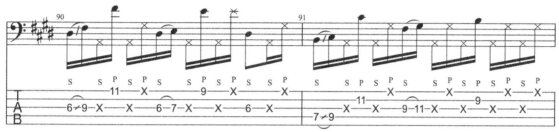

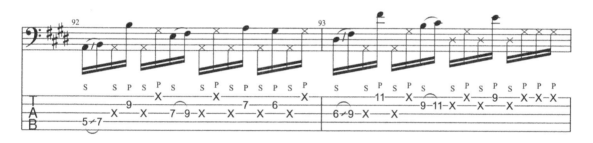

Legion

Video

https://youtu.be/_CR8I6CiOOQ?t=8667

Legion
Nate Navarro

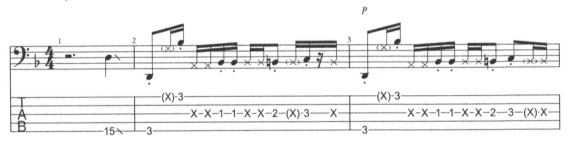

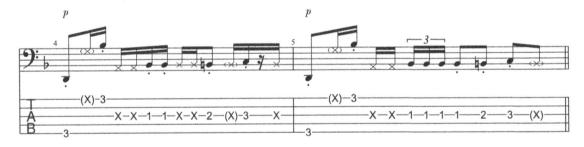

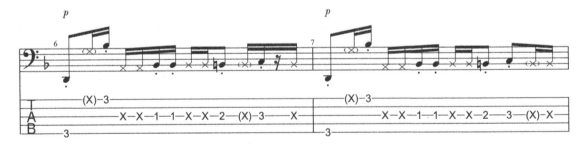

Navarro Music LLC

Bass Trio

Video

https://youtu.be/_CR8I6CiOOQ?t=8782

Bass Trio
Nate Navarro

Standard tuning

♩ = 107

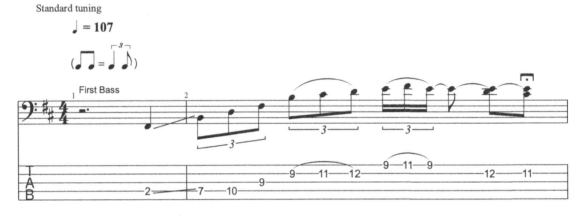

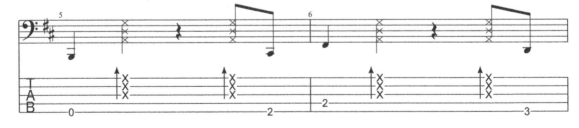

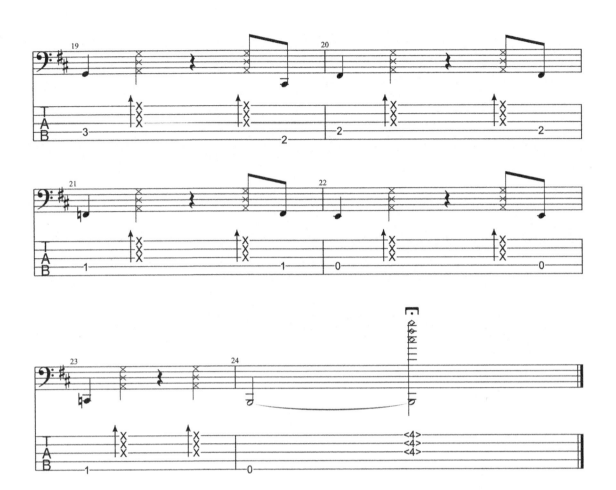

Navarro Music LLC

Bass Trio

Nate Navarro

Standard tuning

♩ = 107

Navarro Music LLC

Songs -
Moderate to Advanced

Bass Trio
Nate Navarro

Songs -
Moderate to Advanced

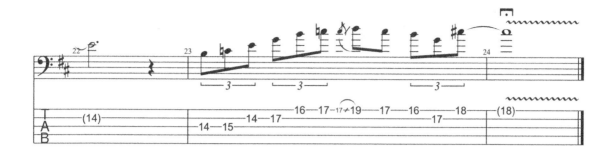

Speed Bag Challenge

Video

https://youtu.be/_CR8I6CiOOQ?t=8849

Speed Bag Challenge
Nate Navarro

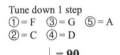

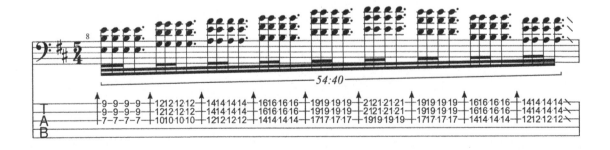

Songs -
Moderate to Advanced

Navarro Music LLC

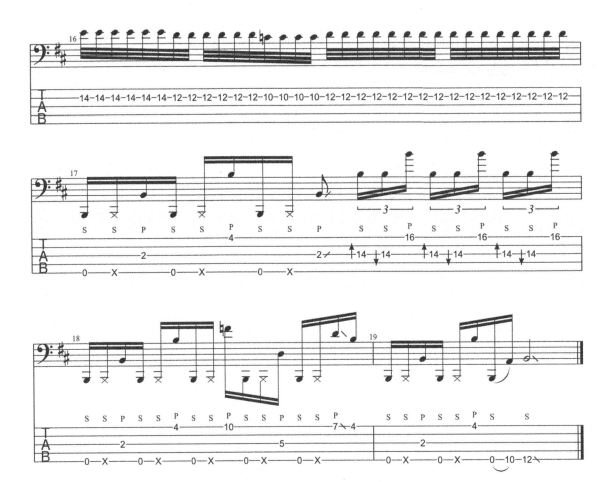

Empath

Video

https://www.youtube.com/watch?v=uIt0rzrbHCA

Empath
Live Bass Solo with Devin Townsend
Nate Navarro

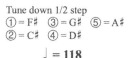

Navarro Music LLC

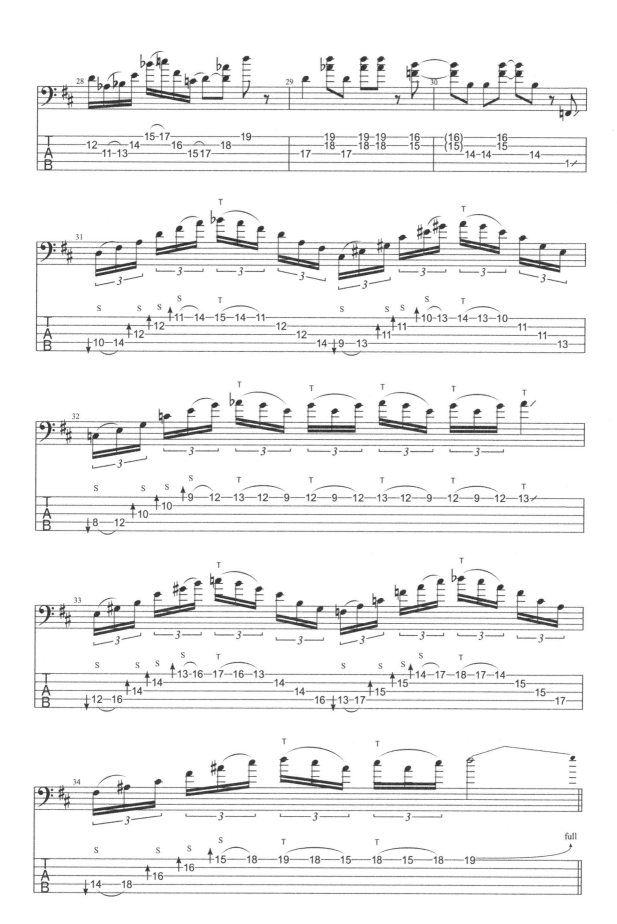

Navarro Music LLC

Additional Online Learning Materials

Moderate to Advanced

Check out the **Easy, Medium, and Hard Bass Tabs** playlists for a frequently updated selection of popular songs with play-along bass tabs right in the video.

Easy

YT: Easy Bass Tabs Playlist by Nate Navarro
URL: https://bit.ly/easybasstabs

Medium

YT: Medium Bass Tabs Playlist by Nate Navarro
URL: https://bit.ly/mediumbasstabs

Hard

YT: Hard Bass Tabs Playlist by Nate Navarro
URL: https://bit.ly/hardbasstabs

Additional Materials

Made in the USA
Coppell, TX
21 November 2024

40715660R00129